Making Sense of the Fine Print

Second Edition

How Today's Front Page Legal Issues
Impact Business, Policy and Personal Success

Newsletters by Thomas L. Fraser

All of the newsletters in this collection were originally published individually by Thomas L. Fraser. The original publication date of each newsletter is given at the beginning of each piece.

Making Sense of the Fine Print : How Today's Front Page Legal Issues Impact Business, Policy and Personal Success : Newsletters by Thomas L. Fraser / written and edited by Thomas L. Fraser

Second Edition: April 2016

ISBN: 0692350748
ISBN-13: 978-0692350744

Library of Congress Control Number: 2015902246

Thomas L. Fraser, New York, New York

Printed in the United States of America

2 4 6 8 10 9 7 5 3

www.tlfraser.com

Go to bed a little wiser than when you woke up.

— Charlie Munger

CONTENTS

Building Companies to Succeed

New Podcast

A Warren Buffett and Charles Munger Book List

LETTER TO READERS

With the publication of this second edition of ***Making Sense of the Fine Print***, I am pleased not only to include new newsletters written since this book was first published in March 2015, but also to announce the launch of my new podcast series. A number of important and noteworthy things have happened in business, law and policy this past year and I appreciate your interest in these important front page topics.

In my podcast, I discuss timely, important front page business and legal issues and interview thoughtful, inspiring people. One purpose of my podcast is to help listeners understand the significance of current issues and how insights from the front pages can be applied to their business and personal lives in valuable ways. In early episodes of my podcast I look at innovation and brand building in China, Jack Ma's letter to shareholders of Alibaba and three noteworthy examples of people providing leadership in volunteering and philanthropy. Expect to hear interviews with some very interesting people in coming weeks.[1]

Warren Buffett and Charles Munger's public commentary has been as sharp and as insightful as ever since this book was first published, so I include in this edition several new pieces about what can be learned about investing, business and life from them. In a podcast recorded in Omaha shortly before this book went to press, I spoke with Jim Ross, proprietor of the Hudson Booksellers bookstore, about books Buffett and Munger read and recommend. The interview is instructive about how smart people become smarter and about the value of continual learning and a lifetime of rich, rewarding reading. The annual letter to shareholders Warren Buffett and Charles Munger wrote to commemorate the 50 years Buffett has led Berkshire Hathaway is, I feel, their best yet. Their observations in this annual letter about the value of continually refining how you invest, focus and culture are worth close consideration.[2]

---

[1] To listen to my podcast, please go to: www.tlfraser.com.

[2] Full disclosure: I am a big fan of Warren Buffett and Charles Munger and a shareholder of Berkshire Hathaway.

The ongoing emergence of China as an economic and political powerhouse is another headline issue on which I focus. Business, political and legal developments in China impact not only the world's second largest economy, but also the global economy. As I discuss in my newsletter and podcast, new business initiatives and policy reforms in China have important implications far beyond Beijing, Shanghai and Shenzhen. I will be writing more about China in coming months.

In this time of rapid transformation and significant new opportunities, one segment of the U.S. economy that is experiencing considerable growth and change is the nonprofit sector. The nonprofit sector in the United States is larger than many people realize. The value of goods and services provided by U.S. nonprofit organizations is approximately 5.5% of gross domestic product. In addition to providing valuable goods and services, nonprofits are creating jobs and providing new sources of economic dynamism. In one of the most extensively researched newsletters in this collection, I describe a variety of steps governments and policymakers can take to encourage the development of nonprofit and charitable organizations in their home countries. It is interesting to note that several major countries have taken important steps in the past year to promote the development of their nonprofit sectors.

It is noteworthy how quickly the fortunes of individual companies and entire country economies can be improved when a touch of vision and intelligent, well-considered laws, policies and management practices are put in place. During the course of the four years these newsletters cover, the United States economy has strengthened significantly and many companies have made impressive gains. I am very bullish about the future and all that can be accomplished in the next few years.

The newsletters collected in this book are presented in their original form and reflect my opinions as of the date they were written. The newsletters have been edited only for purposes of clarification and to take out repetitive text. The transcript of the podcast included in this collection has been edited for clarity and brevity. This book will be updated periodically in the future to include new newsletters and transcripts of selected new podcasts.

The response to my newsletters and podcasts has been greater than I anticipated. Readers and listeners now include Chief Executive Officers,

General Counsels, Senior Policymakers, Entrepreneurs, Philanthropists and others living in five continents. I am delighted and humbled by this response.

To my regular readers and listeners … Thank you again for your questions, comments and observations. I am fortunate to have you as such insightful and inspiring clients, colleagues, readers and friends.

Thomas L. Fraser
New York City
April 7, 2016

.

THE UNITED STATES-KOREA FREE TRADE AGREEMENT

AN OVERVIEW OF THE AGREEMENT AND THE OPPORTUNITIES IT CREATES

Introduction

The Republic of Korea-United States Free Trade Agreement (KORUS FTA)[3] is a free trade agreement between the United States and the Republic of Korea. The Free Trade Agreement was ratified by the United States Congress on October 12, 2011 and signed by President Barack Obama on October 21, 2011. Ratification of the Free Trade Agreement by Korea is pending. The Free Trade Agreement could take effect as soon as January 2012, subject to necessary actions by both countries.

The economic impact of the KORUS FTA could be significant. The U.S. International Trade Commission (the U.S. ITC) has estimated that the Free Trade Agreement would increase U.S. merchandise exports to Korea by as much as $10.9 billion and Korean merchandise exports to the U.S. by as much as $6.9 billion during the first year the Agreement is in effect.[4] The U.S. ITC has also estimated that the Free Trade Agreement would create at least 70,000 new jobs in the U.S. The Free Trade Agreement covers substantially all trade between Korea and the U.S. in goods, services and

---

[3] Office of the United States Trade Representative, "Free Trade Agreement Between The United States of America And The Republic of Korea." Available at: http://www.ustr.gov/trade-agreements/free-trade-agreements/korus-fta/final-text (November 7, 2011).
[4] United States International Trade Commission, "U.S.-Korea Free Trade Agreement: Potential Economy-wide and Selected Sectoral Effects" (September 2007; revised March 2010) (the U.S. ITC Report). Available at: http://www.usitc.gov/publications/pub3949.pdf (November 7, 2011).

agriculture. Under the Free Trade Agreement, nearly 95% of bilateral trade in consumer and industrial products will become duty-free within five years.

The KORUS FTA creates significant new business opportunities in a number of industries. For Korean exporters, the Free Trade Agreement creates important new opportunities in industries including textiles, apparel, motor vehicles and parts, and machinery and equipment. For U.S. exporters, the Free Trade Agreement creates important new opportunities in industries including machinery and equipment, chemicals, rubber and plastic products, agricultural products, and the automotive sector.

This newsletter examines legal, regulatory and business implications of the KORUS FTA. The analysis provided in this newsletter is based on the Free Trade Agreement being ratified by Korea in its current form. As such, the analysis provided in this newsletter would be subject to change if the Free Trade Agreement is amended (or not ratified).

THE IMPACT OF THE FREE TRADE AGREEMENT BY BUSINESS SECTOR

The KORUS FTA was negotiated over a period of years and its provisions are highly detailed and complex. The legal, regulatory and business implications of the Free Trade Agreement vary by business sector and are very industry specific. Following is a short summary of some of the Free Trade Agreement's key legal, regulatory and business implications for specific business sectors.

Agriculture

The American Farm Bureau has estimated that U.S. agricultural exports to Korea could increase by more than $1.9 billion once the Free Trade Agreement is fully implemented.[5] The U.S. meat sector (beef, pork and poultry) is expected to especially benefit from the Free Trade Agreement. The U.S. ITC has estimated that the export of beef products to Korea could increase by $0.6-1.8 billion.

---

[5] American Farm Bureau Federation, "Pending Trade Agreements" (March 2011). Available at: http://www.fbactinsider.org/docs/FTA_Backgrounder.pdf (November 7, 2011).

The U.S. ITC has estimated that U.S. exports of agricultural products to Korea would increase as follows:

- U.S. exports of dairy products would increase between 249% and 478%;
- U.S. exports of vegetables, fruits and nuts would increase between 53% and 87%; and
- U.S. exports of processed food products would increase between 37% and 42%.

The U.S. ITC has estimated that Korean exports of agricultural products to the U.S. would increase as follows:

- Korean exports of dairy products would increase between 107% and 258%;
- Korean exports of processed food products would increase between 15% and 17%; and
- Korean exports of vegetable oils would increase between 26% and 47%.

According to the U.S. House of Representatives Report on the United States-Korea Free Trade Agreement Implementation Act (the House Report),[6] U.S. agricultural exports to Korea faced an average tariff of 54% prior to the adoption of the Free Trade Agreement. Korean agricultural exports to the U.S. faced an average tariff of 9%. The Free Trade Agreement will make more than half of current US agriculture exports to Korea by value duty-free immediately upon implementation. The Free Trade Agreement also addresses certain key non-tariff barriers to trade, such as food safety requirements.

Manufacturing

In 2010, the U.S. exported $32 billion in manufactured goods to Korea. According to the Heritage Foundation, Korean manufacturing tariffs were approximately double those of the U.S. prior to the adoption of the Free

---

[6] House Report 112-239 (October 6, 2011). Available at: http://thomas.loc.gov/cgi-bin/cpquery/R?cp112:FLD010:@1(hr239) (November 7, 2011).

Trade Agreement.[7]

The U.S. ITC has estimated that U.S. manufacturing exports to Korea would increase as follows:

- U.S. exports of motor vehicles and parts would increase between 46% and 59%;
- U.S. exports of metal products would increase between 55% and 63%;
- U.S. exports of chemical, rubber and plastic products would increase between 42% and 45%; and
- U.S. exports of machinery and equipment would increase between 36% and 38%.

The U.S. ITC has estimated that Korean manufacturing exports to the U.S. would increase as follows:

- Korean exports of textiles would increase between 86% and 94%;
- Korean exports of apparel would increase between 145% and 175%; and
- Korean exports of chemical, rubber and plastic products would increase between 18% and 19%.

According to the U.S. ITC, increases in Korean exports of leather goods, footwear, textiles and apparel to the U.S. would be largely a result of reductions in relatively high U.S. tariff rates.

According to the House Report, the Free Trade Agreement will significantly lower or eliminate both tariff and non-tariff barriers to U.S. exports of manufactured goods to Korea. Upon implementation, more than 80% of U.S. exports of consumer and industrial products will immediately become duty-free. Virtually all tariffs will be phased out over ten years. U.S. export sectors that will receive immediate duty-free treatment include aircraft, electric equipment, and medical and scientific equipment.

---

[7] Bruce Klingner, The Heritage Foundation, "The U.S.-Korea Trade Deal's Time Has Finally Come" (October 5, 2011). Available at: http://www.heritage.org/Research/Reports/2011/10/The-US-Korea-Trade-Deals-Time-Has-Finally-Come (November 7, 2011).

The Automotive Sector

Under the terms of the Free Trade Agreement, Korea will reduce its tariffs on U.S. motor vehicles and parts and eliminate non-tariff barriers. Korea will immediately cut its tariffs on U.S. automobiles in half and fully eliminate those tariffs after five years. Korea will also immediately cut its tariffs on U.S. electric cars in half and phase out those tariffs over five years. The Free Trade Agreement also addresses non-tariff barriers to U.S. automotive sector exports, including safety and environmental standards.

The U.S. ITC has estimated that the removal of tariffs would lead to an additional $194 million in new U.S. automotive sector exports to Korea. Additionally, the U.S. ITC has estimated that the removal of non-tariff barriers would add an additional $48-66 million in new U.S. automotive sector exports to Korea.

Korean automakers, and especially Korean automotive parts manufacturers, are expected to be big beneficiaries of the Free Trade Agreement. With the tariff on Korean automobile parts being eliminated immediately under the Free Trade Agreement, automobile parts makers such as Hyundai Mobis Co. and Mando Corp. are expected to boost their market share on the basis of increased price competitiveness.[8]

The Services Sector

Unlike the agriculture and manufacturing industries, the services sector is not subject to tariffs. Instead, services industries (such as financial services, law and accounting) experience trade barriers in the form of government policies that cater to domestic businesses and limit foreign competition. In 2009, the U.S. exported $12.9 billion in services to Korea. The Free Trade Agreement will increase regulatory transparency in the services sector and promote services sector liberalization.

The U.S. ITC has estimated that the Free Trade Agreement would most likely generate a substantial increase in U.S. exports of banking, securities,

---

[8] Lee Minji, Yonhap News Agency, "KORUS FTA Big Boon to South Korean Auto Parts Makers" (October 13, 2011). Available at: http://english.yonhapnews.co.kr/business/2011/10/13/98/0501000000AEN201110 13004600320F.HTML (November 7, 2011).

insurance and asset management services to Korea. The U.S. ITC also estimated that significant new exports of financial services from Korea to the U.S. are not anticipated in the near term because the U.S. financial services market is already fairly open and highly competitive. The increased trade in goods between Korea and the United States resulting from the Free Trade Agreement is expected to lead to increased demand for trade finance services in both countries.

Additional Reforms

In addition to eliminating almost all tariffs on trade between the U.S. and Korea, the Free Trade Agreement also reduces or eliminates many non-tariff barriers to trade. Examples of non-tariff barriers to trade include country-specific automobile emissions standards and food safety standards. Also, a more secure and stable investment environment and enhanced intellectual property rights enforcement should increase trade and investment in a wide variety of goods and services. Importantly, in addition to strengthening economic relationships between Korea and the U.S., the Free Trade Agreement is also an important reaffirmation of Washington's strategic engagement in Korea and East Asia.

SUMMARY

The KORUS FTA is an important step forward in strengthening and expanding the economic and strategic relationships between the U.S. and Korea. Given how the elimination of certain high tariffs and non-tariff barriers will fundamentally change the competitiveness and profitability of certain industries, the Free Trade Agreement will create a number of significant new business opportunities in agriculture, manufacturing, the automotive sector and additional business sectors.[9] As a result of these fundamentally changing industry dynamics, there should be significant new opportunities in:

- Corporate lending;
- Trade finance;

---

[9] For additional detail on which U.S. export industries are estimated to benefit most from the KORUS FTA, see Figure 2.2 of the U.S. ITC Report. For additional detail on which Korean export industries are estimated to benefit most from the KORUS FTA, see Figure 2.3 of the U.S. ITC Report.

- Mergers and acquisitions;
- The formation of new joint ventures between Korean and U.S. companies; and
- More U.S. and Korean companies opening new plants and offices in Korea and the U.S. to be closer to new and expanded markets.

In future newsletters, the details of the Free Trade Agreement as they apply to specific industries will be more closely analyzed.

AUTOMOTIVE INDUSTRY PROVISIONS OF THE UNITED STATES-KOREA FREE TRADE AGREEMENT

THE VOLCKER RULE

THE U.S. SUPER COMMITTEE AND DEBT REDUCTION

In this edition of my newsletter, I focus on the legal, regulatory and business implications of the recently ratified Republic of Korea-United States Free Trade Agreement (the KORUS FTA)[10] as it applies to Korea-U.S. trade in the automotive sector. Additionally, I describe recent rulemaking proposals for the Volcker Rule and analyze implications of the U.S. Congressional Super Committee's inability to agree on a debt reduction package.

KORUS FTA IMPLICATIONS FOR UNITED STATES-KOREA AUTOMOBILE TRADE

Introduction

The KORUS FTA is a free trade agreement between the United States and the Republic of Korea. The Free Trade Agreement was ratified by the United States in October 2011 and was ratified by Korea in November 2011. The Free Trade Agreement could take effect in early 2012, subject to necessary actions by both countries.

---

[10] Office of the United States Trade Representative, "Free Trade Agreement Between The United States of America And The Republic of Korea." Available at: http://www.ustr.gov/trade-agreements/free-trade-agreements/korus-fta/final-text (December 9, 2011).

The KORUS FTA has significant legal, regulatory and business implications for passenger vehicle (car and light truck) and auto parts trade between Korea and the U.S. Under the terms of the Free Trade Agreement, the U.S. and Korea will both phase out tariffs on cars over several years. Non-tariff barriers to trade will also be reduced or eliminated. The Free Trade Agreement will create a number of important new business opportunities for Korean and U.S. car, light truck and parts manufacturers and related businesses.

This edition of my newsletter is the second newsletter describing the legal, regulatory and business implications of the KORUS FTA. Edition #1 of my newsletter provided an overview of the Free Trade Agreement and the opportunities it creates in the agriculture, manufacturing, automotive and services business sectors. This edition of my newsletter provides greater detail about the impact of the Free Trade Agreement specifically on U.S.-Korea trade in the automotive sector.

Korean Automotive Exports to the United States

Under the terms of the KORUS FTA, the U.S. tariff of 2.5% on Korean passenger cars will be kept in place for four years and then eliminated in the fifth year the Free Trade Agreement is in effect. The U.S. will phase out the tariff of 2.5% on Korean electric cars in five equal annual stages. Additionally, the U.S. tariff of 25% on Korean light trucks will be kept in place for seven years and then phased out in three equal annual stages. Given that the U.S. tariff on Korean cars will not be completely eliminated until the fifth year of implementation of the Free Trade Agreement (and not until the tenth year for light trucks), most of the impact on U.S. imports of Korea-manufactured passenger vehicles will likely be experienced in the medium to long term, according to the U.S. International Trade Commission (the U.S. ITC).[11]

Korean automakers exported about 562,000 vehicles to the U.S. last year, according to the U.S. ITC. Hyundai and Kia also have U.S. plants that produce some of the vehicles that have helped make them among the fastest-growing automakers in the U.S., with a combined 9% market share

---

[11] United States International Trade Commission, "U.S.-Korea Free Trade Agreement Passenger Vehicle Sector Update" (March 2011). Available at: http://www.usitc.gov/publications/332/pub4220.pdf (December 9, 2011).

this year through October.[12]

The KORUS FTA should also have a meaningful impact on Korean auto parts trade. Industry analysts have predicted that about 5,000 small and medium-sized Korean auto parts manufacturers will be able to expand their presence in the U.S. once the existing tariff on automobile components is abolished under the Free Trade Agreement.[13] The tariff on Korean-made auto parts will be lifted immediately when the Free Trade Agreement takes effect.

United States Automotive Exports to Korea

Under the terms of the KORUS FTA, Korea will immediately cut its tariffs on U.S. passenger cars in half and fully eliminate those tariffs after five years. Korea will also immediately cut its tariffs on U.S. electric cars in half and phase out those tariffs over five years. U.S. cars exported to Korea have been subject to an 8% tariff, so reducing and eliminating the tariff will make U.S.-manufactured cars more cost competitive in Korea.

The KORUS FTA also addresses non-tariff barriers to U.S. automotive exports to Korea. In an exchange of Legal Texts reflecting an agreement concluded on December 3, 2010 (the December 2010 Agreement),[14] the U.S. and Korea specifically addressed safety and environmental standards and other non-tariff barriers to U.S. exports to Korea. Under the terms of the December 2010 Agreement, the U.S. and Korea agreed to increase the number of U.S.-manufactured vehicles produced to meet U.S. safety standards that can be sold in the Korean market, which has different safety standards. The December 2010 Agreement also revised fuel economy and greenhouse gas emissions standards that will apply to U.S.-manufactured

---

[12] Rose Kim, Bloomberg, "Detroit's 'Bulky' Image Means Modest Gains After U.S.-Korea FTA" (November 28, 2011). Available at:
http://www.bloomberg.com/news/2011-11-29/detroit-s-bulky-image-slows-u-s-car-sales-in-korea-from-free-trade-deal.html (December 9, 2011).

[13] Kim Yon-se, The Korea Herald, "Automakers to benefit most from Korea-U.S. FTA" (November 23, 2011). Available at:
http://www.koreaherald.com/national/Detail.jsp?newsMLId=20111123000688 (December 9, 2011).

[14] Office of the United States Trade Representative, "Legal Texts Reflecting December 3, 2010 Agreement." Available at: http://www.ustr.gov/trade-agreements/free-trade-agreements/korus-fta/legal-texts-reflecting-december-3-2010-agreement (December 9, 2011.)

vehicles sold in Korea during 2012-2015.

The U.S. ITC has estimated that the removal of tariffs would lead to an additional $194 million in new U.S. automotive sector exports to Korea. Additionally, the U.S. ITC has estimated that the removal of non-tariff barriers would add an additional $48-66 million in new U.S. automotive sector exports to Korea.

To increase sales and market share in Korea, U.S. automobile manufacturers also need to address consumer preferences and practical considerations specific to the Korean market. Industry experts cite automobile style, fuel efficiency, brand consciousness and the convenience of after-sales maintenance as reasons why Korean consumers exhibit a strong preference for domestically manufactured automobiles. Gasoline prices in Korea are approximately double those in the U.S. Korean manufacturers accounted for 92 percent of the 1.2 million new vehicles registered in Korea last year, compared with 1.1 percent for U.S. manufacturers.[15]

Business Opportunities in the Automotive Sector

The KORUS FTA is an important step forward in strengthening and expanding trade between the U.S. and Korea in the automotive sector. By eliminating tariffs and non-tariff barriers, the Free Trade Agreement will create a number of important new business opportunities for Korean and U.S. car, light truck and parts manufacturers and related businesses. As a result of fundamentally changing automobile industry dynamics, there should be significant new opportunities in:

- Corporate lending;
- Trade finance;
- Mergers and acquisitions;
- The formation of new joint ventures and business relationships between Korean and U.S. companies; and
- More U.S. and Korean companies opening new plants and offices in Korea and the US to be closer to new and expanded markets.

---

[15] Rose Kim, Bloomberg.

Please feel free to contact me if you would like to discuss opportunities created by the KORUS FTA and how the Free Trade Agreement impacts specific areas of business.

THE VOLCKER RULE

The controversial and highly complex Volcker Rule has moved one step closer to implementation. On October 11 and 12, 2011, federal regulatory agencies issued a 298-page Notice of Proposed Rulemaking to implement the Volcker Rule provisions of the Dodd-Frank Wall Street Reform and Consumer Protection Act of 2010 (the Notice of Proposed Rulemaking).[16] While the Notice of Proposed Rulemaking provides greater detail about what the final form of the Volcker Rule should look like, many difficult issues remain to be resolved.

The Volcker Rule has two central provisions. First, the Volcker Rule generally prohibits U.S. banks and bank affiliates, as well as foreign banks with banking operations in the US and their affiliates (banking entities), from engaging in short-term proprietary trading of any security, derivative and certain other financial instruments for a banking entity's own account. Second, the Volcker Rule generally prohibits banking entities from owning, sponsoring or investing in hedge funds or private equity funds. Both of these provisions are subject to complex exemptions.

Proprietary Trading. The Volcker Rule's proprietary trading provisions essentially prohibit a banking entity from engaging in trading activity as a principal in order to profit from short-term price movements. The Volcker Rule permits market making, trading in government securities, hedging and underwriting. Given that proprietary trading activities can take place in numerous places in a banking entity in addition to at easily identifiable proprietary trading desks, one of the most closely watched issues in the Volcker Rule rulemaking process is how federal regulators distinguish between proprietary trading and permitted financial activities.

---

[16] Office of the Comptroller of the Currency (Treasury), Board of Governors of the Federal Reserve System, Federal Deposit Insurance Corporation and Securities and Exchange Commission, "Prohibitions And Restrictions On Proprietary Trading And Certain Interests In, And Relationships With, Hedge Funds And Private Equity Funds." Available at: http://fdic.gov/news/board/2011Octno6.pdf (December 9, 2011).

In the proposed regulations, rather than drawing a "bright line" between prohibited proprietary trading and permitted activities like market making, the federal regulators set out a variety of criteria and metrics to distinguish between proprietary trading and permitted activities throughout a banking entity. While the proprietary trading provisions as currently proposed leave a significant amount of room for interpretation, regulatory officials have privately indicated that they do not want to see market making activity chocked off and that they would seek to take a pragmatic approach to implementing the Volcker Rule.

Hedge Funds and Private Equity Funds. The proposed regulations impose broad restrictions on the ability of banking entities to own, sponsor or invest in hedge funds and private equity funds. Among other significant provisions, the rule generally prohibits banking entities from owning more than 3% of a hedge fund or private equity fund and investing more than 3% of Tier 1 capital in such funds.

The Volcker Rule as currently proposed is vastly more complex than what its namesake, Paul Volcker, former chairman of the U.S. Federal Reserve, originally envisioned. Mr. Volcker originally wrote a three page memorandum to President Barack Obama outlining the rule.

Federal regulatory agencies are seeking comments from the public on all aspects of the Volcker Rule and have included more than 1,300 questions on nearly 400 topics in the Notice of Proposed Rulemaking. Given the amount of uncertainty and ambiguity surrounding the final form of Volcker Rule provisions, the current rulemaking comment period is critical. The details of the final provisions could have significant implications for banking entities' business models. The comment period ends on January 13, 2012.

Given the large number of questions upon which federal regulators are seeking comments, it would not be surprising to see extensive changes in the final form of the Volcker Rule.

THE U.S. SUPER COMMITTEE AND DEBT REDUCTION

Four months ago, Congress signed off on a law that would require $1.2 trillion in automatic spending cuts over 10 years starting in 2013 if members of the Super Committee (a joint committee comprised of members of the Senate and the House of Representatives) were not able to agree on a way to reduce U.S. deficits. Now that the Super Committee has passed its deadline without being able to reach an agreement, some members of Congress are seeking to make changes to the automatic spending cuts.

As mandated by the Budget Control Act of 2011, the $1.2 trillion in automatic spending cuts is to be evenly divided between defense and non-defense spending. The spending cuts would remove $492 billion from domestic programs and $492 billion from the defense budget over ten years. The spending cuts also include $216 in assumed debt service savings. None of the automatic spending cuts are to take effect until 2013, giving Congress more than a year to modify or override the spending cuts. The Budget Control Act also raises the U.S. debt limit in steps by at least $2.1 trillion, which is currently estimated to be sufficient through early 2013.

Republicans have generally been more vocal about changing the composition of the automatic spending cuts in order to shift the reductions away from the Pentagon. Democrats have generally been less willing to consider changes to the automatic spending cuts, since several of their favorite programs, including Social Security, Medicaid and many veterans' benefits and low-income programs, are protected from the spending cuts. President Barack Obama has threatened to veto attempts to undermine the spending reductions.

Credit rating agencies are closely watching the debate over the automatic spending cuts. If the terms of the automatic spending cuts are watered down, the major credit rating agencies have indicated that they could take additional negative action against the U.S. credit rating. With Fitch Ratings having recently lowered its outlook on U.S. debt to negative, all three of the largest credit rating agencies have a negative outlook on U.S. debt.

Given the Super Committee's inability to reach an agreement on deficit reduction and Congress' penchant for procrastination, any final actions on modifying the automatic spending cuts may not occur until well into 2012 and perhaps not until after Presidential and Congressional elections in November 2012. With Republicans and Democrats sharply divided over how to reduce deficits and large automatic spending cuts due to start taking effect in January 2013, it would not be surprising to see a political deal cut to change the composition of the automatic spending cuts during the lame duck period immediately following next November's elections.

ENHANCED PRUDENTIAL STANDARDS FOR LARGE BANKS AND SYSTEMICALLY IMPORTANT NONBANK FINANCIAL COMPANIES

Risk-Based Capital Requirements and Leverage Limits • Risk Management Requirements for Senior Executives, Boards of Directors and Risk Committees • Planning Ahead; Implications

In this edition of my newsletter, I focus on the legal, regulatory and practical implications of the recent proposal by the Board of Governors of the Federal Reserve System (the "Federal Reserve") to strengthen the regulation and supervision of large bank holding companies and systemically important nonbank financial companies.[17]   The Federal Reserve's proposed enhanced prudential standards and early remediation requirements are perhaps the most important part of the Dodd-Frank Wall Street Reform and Consumer Protection Act ("Dodd-Frank"). Given the significance of the Federal Reserve's proposal, I focus this entire newsletter on this topic.

ENHANCED PRUDENTIAL STANDARDS FOR LARGE BANKS AND CERTAIN NONBANK FINANCIAL COMPANIES

The Federal Reserve recently proposed a new set of rules that would strengthen the regulation and supervision of large bank holding companies and systemically important nonbank financial companies. The Proposed

---

[17] Board of Governors of the Federal Reserve System, Proposed Rule, "Enhanced Prudential Standards and Early Remediation Requirements for Covered Companies" (the "Proposed Rules" or the "Proposal"). Available at: http://www.federalregister.gov/articles/2012/01/05/2011-33364/enhanced-prudential-standards-and-early-remediation-requirements-for-covered-companies.

Rules would impose a number of new capital, liquidity and risk management requirements on the largest and most complex U.S. financial companies in order to protect against future financial crises. The Proposed Rules are perhaps the most important part of Dodd-Frank's response to the recent financial crisis and have significant implications for financial system stability and financial industry profitability.

The Proposal is a central component of Dodd-Frank's efforts to address potential threats to financial stability posed by systemically important financial companies. In addition to subjecting the largest banks and certain nonbank financial companies to stringent new capital and liquidity requirements, the Proposed Rules would also establish rigorous new requirements in the areas of leverage, single-counterparty credit exposure, risk management and stress testing. Further, the Proposed Rules would establish an early remediation regime under which certain financial companies that display signs of financial distress or risk management weakness could be subject to early remedial action.

The Proposed Rules would be applicable to U.S. bank holding companies with $50 billion or more in consolidated assets and large nonbank financial companies that have been designated as "systemically important" by the Financial Stability Oversight Council (collectively, "Covered Companies").[18] Some of the Proposed Rules would also be applicable to certain smaller financial institutions.

In general, the Proposal does not cover foreign banking organizations. The Federal Reserve expects to issue a separate proposal shortly that will apply to foreign banks.

Following are short summaries of key provisions:

Risk-Based Capital Requirements and Leverage Limits

The Proposal sets out a two-stage process for the proposed implementation

---

[18] Approximately 30 U.S. bank holding companies have $50 billion or more in consolidated assets and would initially be subject to the Proposed Rules. The Financial Stability Oversight Council (the "FSOC") has not yet determined which nonbank financial companies will initially be designated as systemically important. The first such designations are expected to be made later in 2012.

of enhanced risk-based capital and leverage standards for Covered Companies.

Under the first stage, all Covered Companies (including nonbank Covered Companies) would be required to comply with, and hold capital commensurate with, the requirements of any regulations adopted by the Federal Reserve relating to capital plans and stress tests. Thus, the Proposal would require all Covered Companies to comply with the capital plan rule recently adopted by the Federal Reserve as well as the stress testing requirements in the Proposal. Additionally, nonbank Covered Companies would be required to comply with the same minimum risk-based and leverage capital requirements that apply to Covered Companies that are bank holding companies.[19]

As part of their capital plan, Covered Companies would be required to demonstrate the ability to maintain capital above existing minimum risk-based capital ratios and above a Tier 1 common risk-based capital ratio of 5% under both baseline and stressed conditions over a minimum nine-quarter planning horizon. Covered Companies that are not able to satisfy these requirements would face limitations on or not be permitted to make capital distributions.

Under the second stage, the Federal Reserve indicated that it plans to issue a separate proposal in the future to implement a quantitative, risk-based capital surcharge. The surcharge would be based on the Basel Committee on Banking Supervision's (the "Basel Committee") capital surcharge framework for global systemically important banks ("G-SIBs").[20] The Proposal states that the surcharge would apply to Covered Companies or to a subset of Covered Companies and that the Federal Reserve contemplates

---

[19] I.e., a minimum Tier 1 risk-based capital ratio of 4%, a minimum total risk-based capital ratio of 8% and a minimum Tier 1 leverage ratio of 4%.

[20] Initially, G-SIBs subject to the surcharge under the Basel Committee framework would face a stricter minimum capital requirement of an additional 1% to 2.5%, depending on a determination regarding each bank's systemic importance. A surcharge of 3.5% would be available for use as a means of discouraging banks from becoming even more systemically important. Globally, twenty-nine banks would initially be subject to the G-SIB surcharge. See Basel Committee on Banking Supervision, "Global systemically important banks: Assessment methodology and the additional loss absorbency requirement" (November 2011). Available at: http://www.bis.org/publ/bcbs207.htm.

adopting rules to implement the surcharge in 2014. The surcharge would be phased in from 2016 to 2019.

Liquidity Requirements

Under the terms of the Proposal, Covered Companies would be required to hold a sufficient quantity of unencumbered, highly liquid assets[21] to survive a 30-day liquidity stress scenario. The Proposed Rules would also require that Covered Companies put in place new liquidity monitoring and compliance regimes.

Senior executives, the board of directors and the board's risk committee would be subject to extensive new liquidity risk management and corporate governance requirements under the Proposal. These requirements would include the periodic review and approval of the Covered Company's liquidity risk tolerance and contingency funding plan.

The proposed liquidity rules are extensive and represent the first time that a regulatory liquidity standard would apply to bank holding companies in the U.S. They were proposed in response to the determination that the failure of liquidity risk management practices contributed significantly to the recent financial crisis. The Basel Committee is also currently working on a minimum liquidity rule. The Federal Reserve is planning to implement the Basel Committee's minimum liquidity rule at a later date.

Single-Counterparty Credit Exposure Limits

The Proposal would limit the credit exposure that any Covered Company and its subsidiaries may have, on a consolidated basis, to any single counterparty and its subsidiaries. A more stringent single-counterparty credit limit would be applied to the largest Covered Companies.

---

[21] "Highly liquid assets" would be defined to include cash or securities issued or guaranteed by the U.S. government, a U.S. government agency or a U.S. government-sponsored entity. It would also include any other asset that a Covered Company demonstrates to the satisfaction of the Federal Reserve: (i) has low credit risk and low market risk; (ii) is traded in an active, liquid secondary market; and (iii) is a type of asset that investors have historically purchased in periods of financial market distress. The Federal Reserve indicated that certain "plain vanilla" corporate bonds could satisfy these criteria.

In general, a Covered Company, together with its subsidiaries, would not be permitted to have an aggregate net credit exposure to any single unaffiliated counterparty, together with its subsidiaries, in excess of 25% of the Covered Company's capital stock and surplus. The Proposal would be more stringent with respect to the credit exposures of any Covered Company that is a bank holding company with total consolidated assets of $500 billion or more and with respect to the credit exposures of any nonbank Covered Company (each, a "Major Covered Company"). Under the Proposal, a Major Covered Company, together with its subsidiaries, would not be permitted to have an aggregate net credit exposure to any single unaffiliated Major Covered Company or to any single foreign banking institution of similar size and complexity,[22] together with its subsidiaries, in excess of 10% of the Major Covered Company's capital stock and surplus.

The Proposal includes detailed rules for determining gross and net credit exposures. The limits apply to aggregate net credit exposures.

Risk Management Requirements for Senior Executives, Boards of Directors and Risk Committees

The Proposal would require each Covered Company, as well as all publicly-traded bank holding companies with $10 billion or more in total consolidated assets, to establish a risk committee of its board of directors. The risk committee would be responsible for documenting and overseeing, on an enterprise-wide basis, the risk management practices of the company's worldwide operations. The risk committee would also be responsible for overseeing the integration of risk management and control objectives into management goals and the company's compensation structure.

The Proposal would also require each Covered Company to employ a chief risk officer who reports directly to the risk committee and to the chief executive officer. The chief risk officer must have sufficient expertise, stature and independence within the company to provide the company with an objective assessment of the risks taken by the company.

---

[22] In general, this would be a foreign banking organization that is or is treated as a bank holding company and that has total consolidated assets of $500 billion or more.

The recent financial crisis highlighted the need for large, complex, globally inter-connected financial institutions to have robust, enterprise-wide risk management. Many of the financial institutions that experienced material financial distress or failed during the financial crisis had significant weaknesses in risk management. The objective of the risk management rules, which are far-reaching in nature, is to strengthen risk management at systemically important financial institutions.

Stress Test Requirements

Under the terms of the Proposal, the Federal Reserve would conduct annual supervisory stress tests on Covered Companies. Additionally, each Covered Company would be required to conduct its own company-run stress test on a semi-annual basis. Further, all bank holding companies, savings and loan holding companies and state member banks with total consolidated assets of more than $10 billion would be required to conduct a company-run stress test on an annual basis. The Federal Reserve would publish summaries of the results of the supervisory stress tests and companies would be required to publish summaries of the results of their company-run stress tests.

Each Covered Company would be required to take the results of the Federal Reserve's analysis of stress tests into account in making changes to its capital plan, capital structure, exposures, concentrations and additional things. The results of the supervisory stress tests could also trigger early remedial action.

Debt-to-Equity Limits for Certain Covered Companies

The Proposed Rules would require a Covered Company to maintain a debt-to-equity ratio of no more than 15 to 1 if the FSOC determines that the company poses a grave threat to U.S. financial stability and the debt limit is necessary to mitigate the risk.

Early Remediation

The Proposal would also establish a regime under which certain financial companies that display signs of financial distress or risk management weakness could be subject to early remedial action. The proposed early remediation regime would include four levels of remediation that would increase in stringency as the Covered Company's financial condition deteriorates. The early remediation measures would range from restrictions on capital distributions and acquisitions, to the divestiture of assets and dismissal of management, to the resolution of the financial institution under the orderly liquidation authority.

The objective of the early remediation regime is to identify and address financial distress at a Covered Company to minimize the possibility of its insolvency and potential harm to U.S. financial stability. As the recent financial crisis demonstrated, the financial condition of a large financial organization can deteriorate rapidly. The proposed early remediation rules were drafted with the intention of giving regulators better tools with which to promptly address emerging problems at Covered Companies.

Planning Ahead; Implications

The Proposed Rules are complex, comprehensive and far-reaching in nature. If approved, they will place significant new requirements and responsibilities on senior executives, boards of directors and senior risk personnel and throughout large financial organizations. While the Proposed Rules must still be adopted, senior executives and board members would be well advised to begin thinking about the implications of the Proposed Rules and how they might best plan for their implementation within their organizations.

In assessing the impact of the Proposed Rules on their organizations, senior executives should consider the following:

- The Proposed Rules are complex and potentially impact numerous areas and activities of a financial organization, either directly and indirectly. Thus, it will be very important to dedicate the appropriate personnel, resources and time to the process of identifying all of the parts of a financial organization that are impacted by the Proposed Rules. Once this has been done, it will be equally important to dedicate the appropriate personnel, resources and time to the process of implementing the new requirements.

- Certain Proposed Rules would require extensive new corporate governance actions. For example, the proposed risk management rules would require the establishment of a risk committee of the board of directors and the appointment of at least one risk committee member with risk management expertise commensurate with the company's capital structure, risk profile, complexity and additional factors. Also, many of the Proposed Rules include new review and approval requirements for the board of directors.

- Certain Proposed Rules could require making important new personnel decisions and putting in place new systems and compliance regimes. For example, the proposed liquidity rules represent the first time a regulatory liquidity standard would apply to U.S. bank holding companies. The budget needed for qualified people and systems to implement a new liquidity regime could be significant. Additionally, the risk management provisions require the appointment of a highly-qualified chief risk officer.

- Certain Proposed Rules would require extensive changes to compliance policies and operational procedures.

- Successful implementation of many of the Proposed Rules will require effective execution and close interaction with regulators, counterparties, service providers and other third parties.

- Senior executives of newly-designated nonbank Covered Companies would face a number of important decisions relating to capital, corporate governance, risk management, compliance, operations and additional areas and activities impacted by the Proposed Rules. Given that they would be subject to a new regulatory regime, they should be especially mindful about communicating with regulators, service providers and others.

- Given the dynamic nature of federal regulatory agency rulemaking, the appropriate senior executives should be closely monitoring and perhaps participating in the rulemaking process.

Given the size, scope and complexity of the Proposal, senior executives and board members would be well advised to begin familiarizing themselves with the Proposal and its implications early in order to plan ahead most effectively.

The Proposal is one of the key provisions underlying Dodd-Frank's approach to strengthening financial regulation and the financial system. In addition to the Proposed Rules, other principal provisions of Dodd-Frank include the Volcker Rule,[23] the creation of the orderly liquidation authority, the establishment of the FSOC with powers to designate nonbank financial companies for heightened oversight, and enhanced regulation of over-the-counter derivatives and other core financial markets.

The Federal Reserve is seeking comments from the public on all aspects of the Proposal and has included 95 questions within the Proposal. The details of the final rules will have important implications for financial institutions' business models, cost of funding, amount of lending, compensation practices, expenses (relating to compliance, operations and additional areas) and profitability. Thus, the comment period and rulemaking are very important. The comment period ends March 31, 2012.

---

[23] To read more about the Volcker Rule, please see Edition #2 of my newsletter (December 12, 2011).

WARREN BUFFETT'S ANNUAL LETTER TO SHAREHOLDERS

UNITED STATES-KOREA FREE TRADE AGREEMENT ENTERS INTO FORCE

In this edition of my newsletter, I focus on several of the legal and business insights that can be gleaned from Warren Buffett's annual letter to shareholders of Berkshire Hathaway. As many of you know, I am a big fan of Buffett and his judgment, independent mindset and common sense. Additionally, in keeping with my focus on providing insight into how changes in laws and regulations create new business opportunities, I comment on the implications of the Republic of Korea-United States Free Trade Agreement (the KORUS FTA), which entered into force March 15.

WARREN BUFFETT'S ANNUAL LETTER:
BOARD PRIORITIES AND FIDUCIARY DUTY

I always look forward to reading Warren Buffett's annual letter to the shareholders of Berkshire Hathaway. This year is no exception. In this year's letter,[24] one sentence in particular caught my attention:

> The primary job of a Board of Directors is to see that the right people are running the business and to be sure that the next generation of leaders is identified and ready to take over *tomorrow*.

---

[24] Warren Buffett's annual letter to shareholders of Berkshire Hathaway is available at: http://www.berkshirehathaway.com/letters/2011ltr.pdf. The complete 2011 Berkshire Hathaway annual report is available at: http://www.berkshirehathaway.com/2011ar/2011ar.pdf.

As usual, Buffett gets it just right. At a time when so many boards of directors are spending so much time on short-term issues and the latest crisis (and doing little or nothing with respect to identifying and grooming future leadership), Buffett and his board are looking ahead and planning for Berkshire Hathaway's future, including the time in the (hopefully distant) future when Buffett is no longer leading the company. This disciplined focus on the big picture and on fundamentals is one of the main reasons why Buffett is so successful as an investor and Berkshire Hathaway is so successful as a company.

In order to fulfill their fiduciary duty, boards of directors need a similar disciplined focus. Every director owes a fiduciary duty to the corporation on whose board he or she sits. This duty includes always acting in the best interests of the corporation. By focusing on management and succession planning (and a few additional key areas), Berkshire Hathaway's board provides an excellent example of how a board should address its fiduciary duty and its overall oversight responsibilities.

In his annual letter, Buffett lavishes praise on portfolio managers Todd Combs and Ted Weschler (they have "brains, judgment and character") and on CEOs Ajit Jain, Tony Nicely, Matt Rose, Greg Abel and Tad Montross, among others. No doubt, lavishing praise on people who deliver outstanding results is great for morale. Buffett is coy about who his designated successor is, only stating that Berkshire Hathaway's board has agreed upon a successor "whose managerial and human qualities they admire" and two superb back-up candidates. Consistent with Buffett's long-term, in-depth, personal approach to strategic decision making, he notes that Berkshire Hathaway's board has had a "great deal of exposure" to his designated successor.

Ultimately, focusing on management and succession is not only an excellent business practice, it is also excellent an legal practice. When a company has the right, highly competent people in place, it will operate more smoothly and most likely have fewer legal and regulatory issues with which to contend. When the right people are in place, the legal and regulatory issues that do inevitably emerge will be resolved more quickly and efficiently. Get the right people in place and you develop a culture that generates success more easily and consistently.

IMPLEMENTATION OF THE UNITED STATES-KOREA FREE TRADE AGREEMENT

The KORUS FTA[25] entered into force March 15. Now that the long-anticipated Free Trade Agreement has become effective, thousands of tariffs on exports between the U.S. and Korea have been reduced or eliminated, non-tariff barriers have come down and new protections have been put in place for exporters, investors and intellectual property rights holders.

The KORUS FTA is the United States' most commercially significant free trade agreement in nearly 20 years. The U.S. International Trade Commission (the U.S. ITC) has estimated that the Free Trade Agreement will increase U.S. merchandise exports to Korea by as much as $10.9 billion and Korean merchandise exports to the U.S. by as much as $6.9 billion during the first year the agreement is in effect.[26] The U.S. ITC has also estimated that increased U.S. merchandise exports to Korea will create at least 70,000 new jobs in the U.S., with additional jobs being created from the further opening of Korea's large services market to U.S. firms. The Free Trade Agreement is expected to make a significant contribution to export expansion and job creation in Korea, as well as helping make Korea's services sector more competitive globally.

The KORUS FTA covers substantially all trade between Korea and the U.S. in goods, services and agriculture. Under the Free Trade Agreement, nearly 95% of bilateral trade in consumer and industrial products will become duty-free within five years.

The KORUS FTA creates a number of important new business opportunities. A few of the most significant opportunities are discussed below.

---

[25] Office of the United States Trade Representative, "Free Trade Agreement Between The United States of America And The Republic of Korea." Available at: http://www.ustr.gov/trade-agreements/free-trade-agreements/korus-fta/final-text.

[26] United States International Trade Commission, "U.S.-Korea Free Trade Agreement: Potential Economy-wide and Selected Sectoral Effects" (September 2007; revised March 2010) (the US ITC Report). Available at: http://www.usitc.gov/publications/pub3949.pdf.

Automobiles

Korean automobile manufacturers, and especially Korean automotive parts manufacturers, are expected to be big beneficiaries under the KORUS FTA. With the tariff on Korean automobile parts being eliminated immediately under the Free Trade Agreement, Korean automobile parts makers are expected to boost their market share on the basis of increased price competitiveness.

Manufacturing

With the implementation of the KORUS FTA, almost 80% of U.S. exports of industrial products to Korea are now duty-free. These products include aerospace equipment, chemicals, electrical equipment and scientific equipment. For Korean manufacturers, the Free Trade Agreement creates important new opportunities in industries including textiles, apparel, and machinery and equipment.

Agriculture

U.S. food producers are big winners under the KORUS FTA. US beef, pork and poultry producers are expected to especially benefit from the Free Trade Agreement. U.S. agricultural exports to Korea faced an average tariff of 54% prior to the adoption of the Free Trade Agreement. With the implementation of the Free Trade Agreement, more than half of U.S. agriculture exports to Korea by value are now duty-free.

Services

Unlike the automobile, manufacturing and agriculture industries, the services sector is not subject to tariffs. Instead, services industries (such as banking, insurance, law and accounting) experience trade barriers in the form of government policies that cater to domestic businesses and limit foreign competition. The U.S. ITC has estimated that the KORUS FTA will most likely generate a substantial increase in U.S. exports to Korea of banking, securities, insurance and asset management services. Given that U.S. financial services markets are already fairly open and highly competitive, significant new exports of financial services from Korea to the U.S. are not anticipated in the near term.

28

Business Opportunities

By eliminating tariffs and non-tariff barriers, the KORUS FTA will create a number of significant new business opportunities in the automotive sector, manufacturing, agriculture, services and additional business sectors. As a result of fundamentally changing industry dynamics, there should be significant new opportunities in:

- Exports;
- Imports;
- Corporate lending;
- Trade finance;
- Mergers and acquisitions;
- Private equity investing; and
- The formation of new joint ventures between Korean and U.S. companies.

For additional insight on the KORUS FTA, please see Edition #1 and Edition #2 of my newsletter. Edition #1 provides an overview of the Free Trade Agreement and the business opportunities it creates. Edition #2 provides insight on the implications of the Free Trade Agreement for U.S.-Korea trade in the automotive sector.

BUFFETT, MUNGER ADDRESS THE IMPORTANCE OF RISK MANAGEMENT AT THE BERKSHIRE HATHAWAY ANNUAL MEETING

Buffett Targets Korea, Japan, Additional Countries in Asia for Expansion

JPMORGAN'S $2 BILLION LOSS AND ITS IMPACT ON THE VOLCKER RULE DEBATE

JAMIE DIMON'S ANNUAL LETTER TO SHAREHOLDERS OF JPMORGAN

In this edition of my newsletter, I focus on several legal and business insights that can be gleaned from Warren Buffett's and Charlie Munger's comments at the Berkshire Hathaway annual meeting. Buffett's and Munger's observations on risk management are especially noteworthy this year. Next, I analyze JPMorgan Chase's $2 billion trading loss and its impact on the debate surrounding the controversial Volcker Rule. Finally, I discuss Jamie Dimon's annual letter to shareholders of JPMorgan Chase and the insight it provides on the cost and complexity of financial regulation in the United States.

BUFFETT: RISK MANAGEMENT IS NOT TO BE DELEGATED

I always learn something valuable from Chairman Warren Buffett's and Vice Chairman Charlie Munger's comments at the Berkshire Hathaway annual meeting. This year was no exception. One of the over-arching themes of their comments during their six-hour question and answer period this year was risk management.

Carol Loomis of Fortune magazine introduced the topic by asking an important question: Will the next Berkshire Hathaway CEO have a separate Chief Risk Officer?

Buffett answered that overseeing risk is a serious job, one that is not to be delegated. "I am the Chief Risk Officer at Berkshire," he said, "and it's on me to make sure we don't get into any catastrophic risk in any way." Understanding risk, he added, is as important as allocating capital and selecting managers.

As a practical matter, Buffett said that understanding risk at Berkshire Hathaway means ensuring that the company does not have too much leverage or insurance risk. Buffett's fundamental investment philosophy also addresses risk management by requiring that investments have a "margin of safety." Thorough risk management also takes into account a variety of additional risks, including market risk, liquidity risk, and legal and compliance risks.

Just as risk management is the responsibility of the CEO and should never be delegated, setting the tone of a company with respect to legal and compliance issues should also be the responsibility of the CEO. CEOs and senior managers lead by example. The CEO is the person who most directly shapes and influences an organization's culture with respect to all business practices, including the organization's attitude toward legal and compliance issues. If the CEO demonstrates by his or her actions that legal and compliance issues are important, then that attitude will permeate the organization. If you are looking for an organization whose CEO takes legal and compliance issues very seriously, look no further than Berkshire Hathaway.

In my law practice, I work with clients on risk management issues, including identifying, anticipating and addressing legal, compliance and business risk exposure.

Buffett Targets Korea, Japan, Additional Countries in Asia for Expansion

One strategic insight that emerged from the annual meeting is that Buffett and the CEOs of some of the companies Berkshire Hathaway owns are targeting markets in Asia for growth and expansion. "Korea, Japan and you name it," Buffett said. Asia – home to several of the world's fastest growing major economies, including China and India – has become a focus for Berkshire Hathaway subsidiaries seeking new markets.

Berkshire Hathaway's reinsurance unit has done "far more business in Asia" in recent months than it did a few years ago, Buffett said. International Dairy Queen, Inc., the ice cream and fast food restaurant chain, recently opened its 500th store in China and has expanded into Singapore. The Lubrizol Corporation, the specialty chemical company, is building a manufacturing plant in the Zhuhai Gaolan Port Economic Zone in southern China. NetJets Inc., the private jet company, recently announced that it will form a joint venture in China to serve the rapidly-growing China market.

While it is common for businesses to chase the newest and most visible opportunities, one characteristic that is common among these investments is that they are all strategic and intended for the long term. No faddish investments here. Buffett is well known for stressing the importance of keeping to your "circle of competence" with respect to investing and only working with people you trust, respect and admire. When investing for growth and expansion in new foreign markets, adhering to these fundamental business principles is as important as ever.

On a practical level, keeping to your circle of competence when investing abroad means a number of things. For example, thorough market research and analysis are just as important in a new country market as they are at home. The local legal, regulatory and tax environment needs to be well understood. Business partners need to be thoroughly vetted. Products or services may need to be modified to suit local preferences.[27] Independent thought and intelligent, focused investing are just as important abroad as they are at home.

In keeping with my focus on providing insight into how changes in laws and regulations create new business opportunities, I am closely monitoring legal and regulatory developments relating to business and investment in

---

[27] For example, International Dairy Queen found that it needed to modify its menu in China. The green tea and green tea almond Blizzards are now the top selling items on its menu in China.

several key countries in Asia. I have worked with clients on business expansion into a number of markets in Asia, Europe and Latin America.

JPMORGAN'S $2 BILLION LOSS AND ITS IMPACT ON THE VOLCKER RULE DEBATE

For much of 2012, the financial industry seemed to be winning the debate over the final details of the Volcker Rule. But that changed with JPMorgan's recent disclosure that it had a $2 billion trading loss in the bank's chief investment office, a supposedly safe part of the business. The $2 billion loss has heightened calls for a stricter Volcker Rule.

Last October, federal regulatory agencies issued a 298-page Notice of Proposed Rulemaking to implement the Volcker Rule provisions of the Dodd-Frank Wall Street Reform and Consumer Protection Act of 2010 (the Notice of Proposed Rulemaking).[28] While the Notice of Proposed Rulemaking provides greater detail about what the final form of the Volcker Rule should look like, it left many difficult issues to be resolved. These issues have been the subject of a fierce debate ever since.

As proposed, the Volcker Rule's proprietary trading provisions would place a number of restrictions on the ability of banking entities to engage in proprietary trading. The Volcker Rule would permit market making, trading in government securities, hedging and underwriting, subject to a number of restrictions. One of the most closely watched issues in the ongoing Volcker Rule rulemaking process is how broadly or narrowly federal regulators define permitted hedging activity to offset risk.

Not all of the facts concerning JPMorgan's hedging strategy have been made public, so it is unclear whether the trading activity would have been considered to come within the Volcker Rule, in its current form. Under the Volcker Rule, as drafted, the first step of analysis is whether a banking entity engaged in proprietary trading under the Volcker Rule. If the activity is proprietary trading, the next step of analysis is whether the

---

[28] Office of the Comptroller of the Currency (Treasury), Board of Governors of the Federal Reserve System, Federal Deposit Insurance Corporation and Securities and Exchange Commission, "Prohibitions And Restrictions On Proprietary Trading And Certain Interests In, And Relationships With, Hedge Funds And Private Equity Funds." Available at: http://fdic.gov/news/board/2011Octno6.pdf.

activity is explicitly permitted under the Volcker Rule. Certain types of risk mitigating hedging activities are permitted under the current version of the rule.

With a balance sheet of $2.3 trillion and capital levels among the best in the business, it is doubtful that the $2 billion trading loss will prove to be a serious blow to JPMorgan (although some hedge fund managers believe that JPMorgan's losses are growing and are betting against its positions). But the trading loss does further complicate the already contentious Volcker Rule debate.

Banks Given Two Years to Fully Comply with the Volcker Rule

A few weeks before JPMorgan's $2 billion loss was disclosed, the Federal Reserve and four other federal regulatory agencies announced that banks and other financial institutions subject to the Volcker Rule will have until at least July 2014 to fully conform their activities and investments to the rule.[29] During the two year conformance period, banks are expected to make good faith planning efforts to enable them to conform to the Volcker Rule.

The clarification was in response to financial industry concern that they would not be able to meet the deadline for compliance with the Volcker Rule. Previous ambiguous regulatory language had advised banks that they had to be in compliance with the Volcker Rule "as soon as practicable" after the July 21 statutory effectiveness date. Federal regulators have been saying for several months that they will probably miss the July 21 deadline for having finalized the details of the Volcker Rule.

Part of the reason rulemaking for the Volcker Rule has been so prolonged is that five federal regulatory agencies – the Federal Reserve, the Securities and Exchange Commission, the Federal Deposit Insurance Corporation, the Commodity Futures Trading Commission and the Office of the Comptroller of the Currency – are involved in writing the rule. The five regulators received more than 17,000 comment letters on the controversial rule.

---

[29] Board of Governors of the Federal Reserve System, "Volcker Rule Conformance Period Clarified." Available at:
http://www.federalreserve.gov/newsevents/press/bcreg/20120419a.htm.

In their announcement, regulators reserved the right to extend the two year conformance period.

JAMIE DIMON'S ANNUAL LETTER TO SHAREHOLDERS OF JPMORGAN

JPMorgan's Cost of Complying with New Regulatory Requirements Put at $3 Billion Over the Next Few Years

Jamie Dimon, the Chairman and Chief Executive Officer of JPMorgan Chase, is known for writing a far-ranging and thought-provoking annual letter to shareholders. A few weeks before JPMorgan's trading loss was disclosed, Dimon's 38-page annual letter[30] accompanying the 2011 annual report was released. Dimon's most recent annual letter is noteworthy for a couple of major reasons.

First, Dimon's annual letter contains some good news. "Housing is getting better." With the economy improving, more jobs being created, more households being formed, the U.S. population continuing to increase and better housing affordability, Dimon's letter states that "the turn [in the housing market] is coming if it is not here already." (Warren Buffet has said that if he could, he would buy up millions of single family homes.)

Second, Dimon's annual letter is noteworthy for what it says about financial regulation. The letter states that it has been estimated that there are 14,000 new regulatory requirements that will be implemented over the next few years. The compliance costs for JPMorgan are huge. "Over the next few years, we estimate that tens of thousands of our people will work on these changes, of whom 3,000 will be devoted full time to the effort, at a cost of close to $3 billion."

While Dimon states that he agrees with the intent of most of the financial reforms passed by Congress, he notes that "the result of the financial reform has not been intelligent design." Some of the regulatory reforms are

---

[30] The Chairman and CEO letter to shareholders of JPMorgan Chase is available at: http://files.shareholder.com/downloads/ONE/1839274153x0x556144/cafb598e-ee88-43ee-a7d3-70673d5791a1/JPMC_2011_annual_report_lTetter.pdf. The complete JPMorgan Chase 2011 annual report is available at: http://files.shareholder.com/downloads/ONE/1839294265x0x556139/75b4bd59-02e7-4495-a84c-06e0b19d6990/JPMC_2011_annual_report_complete.pdf.

inconsistent with each other and hundreds are uncoordinated. "Simplicity, clarity and speed would be better for the system and better for the economy."[31]

To get a sense of just how complex and overlapping financial regulation is in the United States, be sure to take a look at the chart depicting federal regulatory agencies and their lines of authority on page 20 of Dimon's annual letter.[32]

---

[31] Due to space limitations, only a limited amount of Dimon's letter can be analyzed in this newsletter. But it is interesting to note that Dimon's letter states that the cost of credit will go up modestly, in general, "essentially due to banks' higher capital and liquidity requirements." The letter adds that the cost of credit for trade finance, consumers with low credit scores and backup lines of credit may go up more substantially.

[32] The link to Dimon's annual letter is provided in footnote 29.

THE LONDON INTERBANK OFFERED RATE

Recent Libor Issues and Why Libor Is Important • Litigation Issues • Practical Considerations for Decision Makers • What Comes Next? Recommendations for Reforming Libor and Other Global Benchmarks

In this edition of my newsletter, I focus on several of the significant issues currently surrounding the London Interbank Offered Rate (Libor). In June, Barclays agreed to pay U.S. and U.K. authorities £290 million ($453 million) to settle allegations that it had attempted to manipulate Libor. At least 15 additional financial institutions are being investigated. The actions raise a number of important questions regarding the future of Libor and other benchmark interest rates. Libor is the most widely used benchmark for short-term interest rates globally.   As I conclude, the ongoing governmental inquiries into global benchmarks will have significant implications far beyond Libor.

RECENT LIBOR ISSUES AND WHY LIBOR IS IMPORTANT

Until the Barclays settlement, Libor did not receive a lot of public attention. But with the settlement, Libor and similar global benchmarks have been receiving significant attention from regulators, politicians, prosecutors, bankers and borrowers around the world.   At least 10 authorities in three continents are examining issues surrounding Libor and a number of additional global benchmarks, including the Euro Interbank Offered Rate (Euribor) and the Tokyo Interbank Offered Rate (Tibor).

The Barclays settlement highlights two Libor-related issues.   First, authorities are examining whether certain banks colluded to move Libor rates up or down to increase profits or to limit losses on trading positions.

Second, some banks are also being investigated for submitting artificially low interest rates during the financial crisis to makes themselves appear healthier than they might have been. These two issues have raised important questions about the credibility of the Libor rate setting process. The manner in which Libor is structured and calculated is now under close examination.

The Libor Rate Setting Process

Libor refers to a set of interest rate benchmarks set every business day that reflect the cost of funds to banks. Libor is commonly used as a benchmark reference rate for floating rate interest rates. Libor is currently published for ten currencies and 15 maturities ranging from overnight to one year. Libor represents the average cost of unsecured borrowing for banks for a given currency and time period.

Libor is determined based upon the responses of a group of banks to the question:

> At what rate could you borrow funds, were you to do so by asking for and then accepting inter-bank offers in a reasonable market size just prior to 11 am [London time]?

The Libor rate setting process is administered by the British Bankers' Association, an industry trade group. Rates are calculated by Thomson Reuters on behalf of the BBA. The highest and lowest quartiles of submissions are excluded and the average of the remaining submissions determines the Libor rate. Although Libor is calculated in London (hence its name), it is based on daily submissions from a number of international banks and is used as a benchmark globally.

With bank submissions being determined based upon estimates of the rate at which banks could borrow funds in the market, rather than on actual transactions, this approach to calculating Libor has two basic shortcomings. First, this approach raises the risk of rate submissions being manipulated to increase profits or limit losses. Second, banks experiencing financial distress have an incentive to misreport their borrowing rates in order to avoid signaling that they are in trouble.

Most Widely Accepted Global Benchmark

Libor is the most widely accepted benchmark across global financial markets. It was originated in 1986 as a standardized benchmark for use in the syndicated loan market. Since then, its use has expanded to include derivatives and a number of additional types of financial instruments. Libor is commonly used as a benchmark for interest rate swaps, interest rate futures and options, floating rate notes, bank loans, credit cards, student loans, mortgages and other financial instruments. The U.K.'s Wheatley Review of Libor estimated that the notional value of financial products referencing Libor equals at least $300 trillion.

In the United States, there are at least 900,000 home loans indexed to Libor that were originated from 2005 to 2009, a period under investigation. These mortgages carry an unpaid principal balance of approximately $275 billion, according to the U.S. Office of the Comptroller of the Currency. Staff at the Federal Reserve Bank of Cleveland estimated earlier this year that almost 45% of prime adjustable rate mortgages use Libor as their benchmark.

In addition to Barclays, a number of additional banks could be subject to substantial settlements or fines relating to allegations that they had attempted to manipulate Libor. A number of lawsuits have also been filed. Estimates of the potential cost of settlements, fines and litigation vary widely.[33]

THE U.K.'S WHEATLEY REVIEW OF LIBOR

The United Kingdom government has commissioned Martin Wheatley, Managing Director of the Britain's Financial Services Authority and Chief Executive-designate of the Financial Conduct Authority, to undertake a review of Libor. The terms of reference of the Wheatley Review include considering:

---

[33] See, for example, Brooke Masters and Alex Barker, Financial Times, "Banks' Libor costs may hit 22 bn" (July 12, 2012), available at: http://www.ft.com/intl/cms/s/0/0231ace4-cc1d-11e1-839a-00144feabdc0.html#axzz24K3Rpg7l, and David Benoit, The Wall Street Journal, "Libor Scandal: KBW Attempts Estimating Exposures" (July 7, 2012), available at: http://blogs.wsj.com/deals/2012/07/17/libor-scandal-kbw-attempts-estimating-exposures/.

- Whether Libor should be formally regulated;
- Whether Libor should be based on actual trade data rather than on banks' own estimates of the rates at which they could borrow at a given time;
- Whether alternative rate setting processes should be used;
- What the financial stability consequences of a move to a new regime for determining Libor might be and how such a transition could be appropriately managed; and
- Whether sanctions for manipulating Libor should be strengthened.

The Wheatley Review is also considering whether similar measures are required for other global markets and benchmarks.

The Wheatley Review released its initial discussion paper on Libor on August 10.[34] Stakeholders have until September 7 to submit written responses to questions raised in the discussion paper. The Wheatley Review expects to publish its final recommendations by the end of September.

In addition to the Wheatley Review in the U.K., policy makers in other countries are addressing Libor as well. The European Central Bank is scheduled to discuss Libor at a September 9 meeting in Basel, Switzerland. Among others, the U.S. Commodity Futures Trading Commission and the European Union also have Libor projects underway.

LITIGATION ISSUES

Despite the settlement between Barclays and the U.S. and U.K. authorities, it will not be easy for private sector plaintiffs to make a successful Libor case. First, proving liability for actions involved in the calculation of Libor will not be easy. Libor is not, by itself, a price. Rather, Libor is an estimate of the interest rate at which banks would lend to each other. Parties creating a contract are not required to use Libor as a term in their contract. Parties who do use Libor often add additional costs (typically, a credit spread).

---

[34] HM Treasury, "The Wheatley Review into LIBOR: initial discussion paper" (August 2012). Available at: https://www.gov.uk/government/uploads/system/uploads/attachment_data/file/191763/condoc_wheatley_review.pdf.

Second, it will not be easy to establish damages. Establishing the amount of harm done will require, among other things, determining what the Libor rate should have been for individual trading days. Given the level of government intervention in the bank funding market and the scarcity or absence of interbank lending during certain periods, the highly complex task of determining what the Libor rate should have been is made even more difficult.

U.S. District Judge Naomi Reice Buchwald is overseeing several proposed class actions relating to Libor. As of the date of this newsletter, the matters were at a very preliminary stage. The Libor litigation will involve a number of complex legal issues. For more information on the matters before Judge Buchwald, see In re: LIBOR-Based Financial Instruments Antitrust Litigation, 11-MD-2262, U.S. District Court, Southern District of New York (Manhattan).

PRACTICAL CONSIDERATIONS FOR DECISION MAKERS

Given current uncertainties about the future of Libor and certain other benchmarks, many attorneys, executives, board members and other decision makers are facing difficult questions. To put the issues into context, it is important that decision makers be well informed. Thus, they should consider doing the following:

- Determining whether financial assets reference Libor or another benchmark;
- For contracts referencing Libor or another benchmark, determining whether the contracts specify alternative interest rates if Libor or the other benchmark is not published; and
- Considering whether to use a benchmark interest rate like Libor and/or alternative benchmarks in new and future contracts.

Additionally, for firms submitting Libor rate setting information, decision makers should consider performing a Libor-related compliance audit and reviewing the firm's Libor compliance policies and procedures.

Decision makers should keep apprised of benchmark-related regulatory developments, regulatory investigations and litigation potentially affecting their companies and counterparties. Additionally, decision makers should keep informed about changing business practices with respect to Libor and other benchmarks.

Questions relating to existing and new contracts referencing Libor and pending and potential regulatory and private sector actions are complex and specific to each individual company and each individual contract. Readers should seek advice from professional advisers.

WHAT COMES NEXT? RECOMMENDATIONS FOR REFORMING LIBOR

As described above, Libor is deeply imbedded in the global financial system. Trillions of dollars worth of financial instruments and loans to corporations and individuals reference Libor. Thousands and thousands of these contracts that reference Libor have multiple years remaining until maturity. Given the existence of so many contracts tied to Libor, credibility needs to be restored to the Libor rate setting process.

Several steps can be taken to increase market confidence in Libor:

First, to the extent possible, Libor should be based more on actual interbank loans. Currently, Libor is determined based upon estimates of the rate at which banks could borrow funds in the market. Where possible, Libor submissions should be validated by as many actual transactions of a reasonable size as possible. Banks should also be required to document these numbers.

Second, Libor should be focused primarily on the most liquid maturities. Limiting Libor to shorter maturities would enhance Libor's credibility by making it more representative of how bank funding actually works and where transactions actually exist.

Third, more banks should contribute to the Libor rate setting process. Having more banks contribute to the Libor process should reduce the incentive for financially struggling banks to misreport rates to make themselves look healthier than they might be and should make collusion among banks more difficult.

Fourth, Libor should be formally regulated. Currently, Libor is overseen by the British Bankers Association, an industry trade group. But self regulation has not worked. Thus, Libor and other benchmarks should be subject to formal regulatory oversight. The new regulatory regime should require much stronger governance and oversight and much greater independence and transparency in the manner in which Libor and other benchmarks are calculated. Sanctions for manipulating benchmarks should be strengthened. Enhanced regulation and independent audits should go a long way toward restoring confidence in Libor.

Finally, senior managers of financial institutions that submit rate setting information for Libor and similar benchmarks need to closely review (and then continue to closely monitor) how their banks' Libor submissions are determined and submitted. This internal review of banks' involvement in the rate setting process should include a review of who submits Libor information, how rate submissions are determined and whether personal incentives encourage appropriate behavior and oversight. As recent disclosures relating to Libor and other corporate practices are demonstrating, lapses in behavior and oversight can be very expensive, both in financial terms and in terms of individual and corporate reputation. Senior managers and board members should realize that ongoing investments in internal controls, compliance and building a solid corporate culture are time and money well spent.

Alternative Benchmarks

There has been talk of replacing Libor with another benchmark. This talk is likely to remain just talk for two reasons. First, there is no alternative benchmark that would easily work for all the types of financial instruments that currently rely on Libor. Second, rewriting the thousands and thousands of contracts referencing Libor would be a huge and legally problematic undertaking.

Historically, market benchmarks have evolved over time. Benchmarks also come and go. The same is happening now. For example, in the past few years, the Depository Trust & Clearing Corporation GCF Repo Index™ and Overnight Index Swaps have grown as benchmarks serving specific sectors of the short-term funding markets. Neither is a perfect replacement for all of the types of transactions that rely on Libor, but they are examples of how benchmarks gain market credibility and become more broadly relied upon over time.

Over time, alternative benchmarks should develop for some or all of the types of financial instruments that currently rely on Libor. But it takes time for benchmarks to develop and gain credibility. Thus, in the near term, reforming and restoring confidence in Libor will remain a priority.

LESSONS FROM LIBOR FOR THE REFORM
OF OTHER GLOBAL BENCHMARKS

Mindful of the shortcomings identified with Libor, the Wheatley Review and a number of additional regulators and industry groups are examining other global benchmarks. Benchmarks like Libor are prevalent throughout the banking industry and in many additional markets. For example, the Wheatley Review lists 38 global interbank benchmarks.[35] International commodity prices (like the spot oil price) are also examples of global benchmarks.

As inquiries into global benchmarks continue, regulators and industry groups will be looking for, among other things, shortcomings similar to those found with Libor. These weaknesses could include, among other things, a lack of transparency, conflicts of interest and a potential for manipulation. Decision makers of companies submitting rate setting information for or relying upon other global benchmarks are well advised to make inquiries of their own into the particular benchmark. As the broad ambit of the ongoing Wheatley Review is demonstrating, the global debate about benchmarks is no longer just about Libor.

---

[35] For the Wheatley Review's list of global interbank benchmarks, please see Table 5.A. in the initial discussion paper. The link to the paper is provided in footnote 33.

THE LONDON INTERBANK OFFERED RATE

The UK Wheatley Review of Libor: A Summary of Final Recommendations • New Libor Administrator to Be Selected • Implications of the Wheatley Review for Libor and Other Global Benchmarks

In this edition of my newsletter, I focus on the U.K. Wheatley Review of Libor and its recently released recommendations for the reform of the London Interbank Offered Rate (Libor) and similar global benchmarks. In its final report, the Wheatley Review recommended that Libor should be comprehensively reformed, rather than replaced with a new benchmark, and that transaction data should explicitly be used to support submissions from banks submitting Libor rate setting information. The Wheatley Review also recommended that the British Bankers Association (the BBA) transfer administration of Libor to a new administrator.

THE WHEATLEY REVIEW: FINAL RECOMMENDATIONS

Since 2009, the U.K. Financial Services Authority (the FSA) and regulators in a number of additional jurisdictions, including the United States, the European Union, Japan and Switzerland, have been investigating a number of financial institutions for alleged misconduct with respect to Libor and additional global benchmarks. Following the agreement in June by Barclays to pay U.S. and U.K. authorities £290 million ($453 million) to settle allegations that it had attempted to manipulate Libor, the U.K. government asked Martin Wheatley, Managing Director of the FSA and Chief Executive-designate of the new Financial Conduct Authority, to lead an independent review into the setting and usage of Libor.

In its final report,[36] the Wheatley Review makes a number of recommendations about the regulation, governance and structure of Libor to the U.K. Government, the BBA, banks and regulators. The Wheatley Review also makes recommendations relating to other global benchmarks. These recommendations are now subject to action by Parliament and other bodies in the U.K. and in other jurisdictions.

10-Point Plan for the Reform of Libor

The Final Report of the Wheatley Review sets out a 10-point plan for the reform of Libor.[37] Key recommendations include:

- The FSA should regulate the submission and administration of Libor, as well as approve the key persons involved. The FSA should be allowed to prosecute manipulation or attempted manipulation of Libor;
- The BBA should transfer administration of Libor to a new administrator. The new administrator should be responsible for compiling and distributing the rate, as well as for providing credible internal governance and oversight. The transfer should be achieved through a tender process run by an independent committee;
- The new administrator should be responsible for the surveillance and scrutiny of Libor rate submissions, the publication of a statistical digest of rate submissions and the performance of periodic reviews addressing whether Libor continues to meet market needs effectively and credibly;
- Submitting banks should immediately look to comply with the submission guidelines contained in the Final Report, including making explicit use of transaction data to corroborate their submissions;
- The new administrator should introduce a code of conduct for submitting banks. The code of conduct should include guidelines for the use of transaction data to determine submissions and a requirement for regular, external audits of submitting banks;
- The BBA and, in due course, the new administrator, should stop compiling and publishing Libor for currencies and maturities for

---

[36] HM Treasury, "The Wheatley Review of LIBOR: final report" (September 2012) (the Final Report). Available at: https://www.gov.uk/government/uploads/system/uploads/attachment_data/file/191762/wheatley_review_libor_finalreport_280912.pdf.

[37] See pages 8-9 of the Final Report for additional detail on the 10-Point Plan.

which there is insufficient trade data to corroborate submissions. Publication of all Libors for Australian Dollars, Canadian Dollars, Danish Kroner, New Zealand Dollars and Swedish Kronor and for selected maturities should be phased out over a 12-month transition period;

- The publication of bank submissions should be delayed by at least three months to reduce the potential for submitters to attempt manipulation and to reduce the potential interpretation of rate submissions as a sign of creditworthiness;

- Banks, including those not currently making Libor submissions, should be encouraged to participate as widely as possible in the Libor rate setting process. If necessary, banks may be required to participate through new regulation;

- Market participants using Libor should be encouraged to consider whether Libor is the most appropriate benchmark for their transactions and whether their standard contracts contain adequate contingency provisions covering the event of Libor not being produced; and

- The U.K. authorities should work closely with the international community to contribute fully to the debate on the long-term future of Libor and other global benchmarks. This work should include establishing and promoting clear principles for effective global benchmarks.

Given the deep entrenchment of Libor in global financial markets and the potential for financial market disruption if it were replaced, the Wheatley Review decided to recommend reforming Libor rather than replacing it. In its initial discussion paper, the Wheatley Review estimated that the notional value of financial products referencing Libor equals at least $300 trillion globally.[38]

New Libor Administrator to Be Selected

One of the most noteworthy recommendations of the Wheatley Review is that the administration of Libor should be transferred from the BBA to a new administrator. The Wheatley Review concluded that the current

---

[38] For additional background on Libor issues, see: HM Treasury, "The Wheatley Review of LIBOR: initial discussion paper" (August 2012) (available at: https://www.gov.uk/government/uploads/system/uploads/attachment_data/file/191 763/condoc_wheatley_review.pdf) and Edition #6 of my newsletter (August 23, 2012).

administration of Libor suffered from weaknesses in governance, oversight and accountability. The new administrator will be selected through a tender process run by an independence committee.

The new administrator will be responsible for two broad areas of responsibility: compiling and distributing Libor, and internal governance and oversight of Libor.

Key recommendations for the responsibilities of the new administrator and for a reformed governance framework for Libor include:

- The administrator should analyze and scrutinize Libor submissions from contributing banks;
- The governance framework for Libor should include a prominent decision-making and oversight role conducted by an independent and powerful oversight committee with an ability to operate autonomously; and
- The administrator and the oversight committee should develop and implement a code of conduct with industry input outlining detailed policies and procedures that contributing firms and the administrator would be expected to follow.

The new **administrator** will be responsible for the ultimate oversight and operation of all aspects of Libor. Scrutiny of Libor submissions will be a crucial aspect of its responsibilities. The Wheatley Review recommended that such scrutiny should include both pre-publication verification checks, to avoid errors in submissions, as well as post-publication scrutiny against a set of data, including inter-bank and other unsecured deposit transactions, as well as other relevant financial data.

While the new administrator will have ultimate responsibility for all aspects of the governance of Libor, the Wheatley Review recommended that the **oversight committee** be responsible for aspects of Libor internal governance that require input from a wider pool of stakeholders. In particular, the Wheatley Review recommended that the definition and scope of Libor should remain at the discretion of the oversight committee. This would permit a wider pool of stakeholders to ensure that Libor evolves in line with changes in the structure and operation of the financial markets. The oversight committee would also be responsible for helping develop the code of conduct.

The Wheatley Review stated that some aspects of benchmark administration could be undertaken by different institutions. For example, Libor calculation and distribution could be delegated to a different company. However, the Wheatley Review stated that the new administrator should retain overall responsibility for all of the activities of the administrator.

Given that fulfilling the responsibilities of the administrator will be expensive, the Wheatley Review recommended that the new administrator should be permitted to explore ways to commercialize Libor.

The transfer of Libor from the BBA to a new administrator represents a significant business opportunity for the eventual winner. One key to making a successful bid will be presenting a well-thought-through vision for Libor governance, oversight and administration. The old system of Libor administration suffered from a lack of accountability at both the organizational and the individual level. Both will have to be addressed. A successful bid should also creatively and insightfully address how to keep Libor relevant and appropriately evolving in the future.[39]

Libor Submission Guidelines

An additional key recommendation of the Wheatley Review is that Libor submissions should be supported and corroborated by transaction data. Given that it will be some time before the new rule book and a detailed code of conduct can be agreed upon to put this recommendation in place, the Wheatley Review included Libor submission guidelines in the Final Report to use in the interim. The Wheatley Review stated that submitting banks should start using these guidelines immediately in preparing their Libor submissions.

In its submission guidelines, the Wheatley Review stated that Libor submissions should be determined based upon a hierarchy of transaction types. In developing their Libor submissions, submitting banks should

---

[39] For additional detail on the numerous and detailed recommendations of the Wheatley Review for the responsibilities of the administrator and the oversight committee and for additional insight into what should be included in a bid to be administrator, see Paragraphs 3.18-3.37 of the Final Report. The Wheatley Review will be releasing additional guidance about the tender process.

place greatest emphasis on their transactions in the unsecured inter-bank deposit market, followed by transactions in other unsecured deposit markets (including certificates of deposit and commercial paper) and other related markets (including overnight index swaps, repurchase agreements, foreign exchange forwards, interest rate futures and options and central bank operations). Submitting banks should then consider their observations of third party transactions in the same markets and quotes by third parties offered to submitting banks in the same markets. In the absence of transaction data relating to a specific Libor benchmark, submitting banks should then use expert judgment to determine a Libor submission.[40]

Code of Conduct

As mentioned above, one of the new administrator's first and primary responsibilities will be creating a code of conduct for financial institutions involved in the Libor rate setting process. The drafting of the code of conduct will be done by the administrator, through the oversight committee, in collaboration with Libor contributors and market participants. By involving the private sector in developing the code of conduct, the intention is that the governance and oversight of Libor will be dynamic and evolve over time to help keep the benchmark fit for purpose and to help it evolve to meet the changing needs and nature of the market.

Key elements recommended for the code of conduct include:

- Detailed and specific Libor submission guidelines, including guidelines for the use of transaction data to be taken into account when determining submissions;
- Internal systems and control policies for submitting banks, including an outline of individual responsibilities within each firm;
- Record keeping requirements for submitting banks, including records of transactions in inter-bank deposits and other relevant financial instruments; and
- Regular external audit requirements for submitting banks.

The Wheatley Review's recommendations for the code of conduct are numerous and detailed. Additional significant recommendations include

---

[40] For additional detail on the Wheatley Review's Libor submission guidelines, see Paragraphs 4.5-4.11 and Box 4.B. in the Final Report.

conflicts of interest management procedures, annual internal audits, regular compliance reviews, and the physical separation of individuals responsible for Libor submissions from interest rate derivatives traders. The Wheatley Review also recommended the creation of requirements for the corroboration of Libor submissions both internally within the submitting bank and externally by the new administrator and the oversight committee.[41]

New Contracts

One of the challenges facing the Wheatley Review was how to reform Libor to improve its credibility while new financial contracts that reference Libor continue to be written every day. Many of these contracts use definitions, terms and conditions that are standardized across a specific industry. Some forms of contract are better than others about including contingency provisions that adequately address contingencies such as changes to Libor or Libor not being published. Accordingly, the Wheatley Review very appropriately recommended that industry bodies that publish standardized legal documentation referencing Libor, as well as all Libor users, should develop robust contingency procedures to take effect in the event that the publication of Libor is disrupted. New contracts and legal documentation should be drafted to address contingencies including changes to Libor and Libor not being published.[42]

LOOKING AHEAD; IMPLICATIONS OF THE WHEATLEY REVIEW FOR LIBOR AND OTHER GLOBAL BENCHMARKS

During the press conference announcing the recommendations of the Wheatley Review, Martin Wheatley observed that "Libor became the model that every market around the world copied to a greater or lesser degree." Thus, it is important that the recommendations of the Wheatley Review be seriously considered and debated and that the model for the regulation, governance and structure of Libor that emerges be one that is worth emulating.

---

[41] For additional detail on the specific recommendations of the Wheatley Review for the code of conduct, see Paragraphs 4.14-4.31 of the Final Report.

[42] Questions relating to existing and new contracts referencing Libor are complex and specific to each individual company and each individual contract. Readers should seek advice from professional advisers with respect to specific contracts.

Properly implemented, the recommendations of the Wheatley Review should go a long way toward re-establishing confidence and credibility in Libor (and, hopefully, eventually in benchmarks more generally). The Wheatley Review has made a number of excellent recommendations. But the beauty is in the doing and in the details. There is still a lot of hard work to be done.

A broader theme underlying the thoughtful, forward-thinking work of Martin Wheatley and his Wheatley Review colleagues is that regulation, governance and oversight need to constantly and constructively evolve along with the financial markets for which they are responsible. Libor, now referenced in financial products with a notional value of at least $300 trillion globally, has grown dramatically in usage since 1986, when it was introduced to be used as a standardized benchmark in the syndicated loan market. Regulation, governance and oversight need to constantly and thoughtfully evolve to address ongoing and dynamic changes in the marketplace.

TAP DANCING TO WORK: WARREN BUFFETT ON PRACTICALLY EVERYTHING, 1966-2012

QUESTIONS AND ANSWERS WITH CAROL LOOMIS

THE ASSET WARREN BUFFETT VALUES MOST

In this edition of my newsletter, I review Carol Loomis' new book *Tap Dancing to Work: Warren Buffett on Practically Everything, 1966-2012*. *Tap Dancing to Work* is a collection of **Fortune** magazine articles about Warren Buffett with commentary by Loomis. The book presents a fascinating look at Buffett's career to date and covers an important part of recent business history. Loomis, who has been a close friend of Buffett's for more than 40 years, is the chief writer about Buffett at **Fortune** and has edited Buffett's annual letter to shareholders since 1977. In a Question & Answer following, Carol Loomis shares her thoughts on several of the important themes in her book, including Buffett as teacher and the key to the quality of Buffet's annual letter to shareholders.

TAP DANCING TO WORK: A FEW OF THE STEPS

Since first mentioning Buffett in an article about hedge fund pioneer Alfred Winslow Jones in 1966, Loomis and her colleagues at **Fortune** have written a number of articles about Buffett and Berkshire Hathaway. This book contains the best of those articles and includes a dozen pieces written by Buffett himself. Commentary by Loomis provides context and perspective. While much has been written about Buffett, this book contains considerable fresh insight on an always fascinating subject.

While it is not possible to fit Warren Buffett's observations on "practically everything" into this short book review, I would like to touch upon several of the important themes in this excellent and enjoyable book. Before I start, I would like to make the following disclosure: I was born and raised in Nebraska. I started reading about Warren Buffett and Berkshire Hathaway when I was a teenager. I am a fan.

Warren Buffett the Teacher

Much has been written about Warren Buffett the investor and Warren Buffett the business manager. But Warren Buffett the teacher has been less commented upon.

In the article "Gates on Buffett," written by Bill Gates, Gates describes the first time he met Buffett:

> He asked good questions and told educational stories. There's nothing I like so much as learning, and I had never met anyone who thought about business in such a clear way.

Buffett's teaching and his clarity of thinking are probably most widely appreciated through his annual letters to shareholders of Berkshire Hathaway. Buffett began writing the chairman's letter in the annual report in 1966. His annual letters have developed and evolved over the years. His letters are now among the most widely read and closely analyzed and commented upon pieces of writing coming out of corporate America annually.

Buffett's annual letters deal with a variety of topics. In addition to describing typical corporate fare such as Berkshire Hathaway's operating results and major acquisitions for the past year, Buffett's annual letters also address a number of broader themes, including accounting, valuation, stock options, board responsibilities, shareholder rights and Berkshire Hathaway's acquisition philosophy.

Buffett's writing is original, thoughtful, pithy, oftentimes entertaining and always educational. Reading his annual letters provides an education not only on business issues, but also on human nature and common sense.

In his 1987 annual letter, Buffett writes about value investing:

> We really don't see many fundamental differences between the
> purchase of a controlled business and the purchase of marketable
> holdings. In each case we try to buy into businesses with favorable
> long-term economics. Our goal is to find an outstanding business
> at a sensible price, not a mediocre business at a bargain price.

In addition to investing in outstanding businesses at a sensible price,
Buffett also emphasizes investing in businesses managed by quality people.
In his 1989 annual letter he writes:

> … I learned to go into business only with people whom I like, trust
> and admire … an owner—or investor—can accomplish wonders if
> he manages to associate himself with such people in businesses
> that possess decent economic characteristics.

Reading Buffett's annual letter, one gets a good understanding of how
Berkshire Hathaway performed the past year. But Buffett's annual letters
are about much more than just prescribed corporate disclosure. Reading a
series of Buffett's annual letters, one gains significant insight into how a
highly intelligent, creative and disciplined person approaches running a
highly complex, successful company.   The reader sees that Buffett's
investment and management decisions are informed by clearly defined
business priorities, performance criteria and acquisition criteria. Readers
also appreciate how his decisions are informed by a nuanced understanding
of the legal and regulatory environment. With such clear thinking about
fundamental issues, perhaps it is not surprising Buffett is so successful.

In addition to writing a highly educational annual letter, Buffett teaches and
mentors in a variety of other ways. He talks regularly, sometimes daily,
with a number of his CEOs and senior executives. Along with Berkshire
Hathaway Vice Chairman Charlie Munger, he answers hours of questions
at the annual shareholders meeting. He writes occasional op-eds and does
media interviews. And he regularly speaks with groups of business school
students.

As described in Nicholas Varchaver's "What Warren Thinks …," the
student question and answer sessions are wide-ranging. They cover topics
ranging from starting new companies and how Buffett gets his ideas ("I

read all day") to habits and character. During the 2011-2012 school year, 1,450 students took part.

A common question students ask is how Buffett defines personal happiness and success. I especially appreciate Buffett's observations, from "The Bill and Warren Show," edited by Brent Schlender, on this topic:

> ... when you go out to work, work for an organization of people you admire, because it will turn you on.

> I have turned down business deals that were otherwise decent deals because I didn't like the people I would have to work with. I didn't see any sense in pretending. To get involved with people who cause your stomach to churn—I say it's a lot like marrying for money. It's probably a bad idea under any circumstances ...

Asking good questions and telling educational stories are an important part of teaching and learning. CEOs and senior managers are well advised to pursue teaching and mentoring practices like Buffett's. Oftentimes, the teacher learns as much as the student.

Buffett's annual letters are available at the Berkshire Hathaway website.[43] I highly recommend reading them.

(For more on Buffett as teacher, see Loomis' observations in the Question & Answer.)

Warren Buffett the Philanthropist

Philanthropy is an area where big thinking can have big results. In recent years, Buffett and Bill and Melinda Gates have worked together on two highly thoughtful examples of big thinking: Buffett's gift to the Bill &

---

[43] Warren Buffett's annual letters to shareholders of Berkshire Hathaway for the years 1977-2011 are available at:
http://www.berkshirehathaway.com/letters/letters.html. For an explanation of Berkshire Hathaway's broad economic principles of operation, see "Owner-Related Business Principles" at pages 89-94 of the 2009 annual report:
http://www.berkshirehathaway.com/2009ar/2009ar.pdf. For readers who are on audit committees, let me recommend reading Buffett's recommendations for members of audit committees in the 2002 annual letter:
http://www.berkshirehathaway.com/letters/2002pdf.pdf.

Melinda Gates Foundation and the Giving Pledge.

Buffett's huge gift of Berkshire Hathaway stock to the Gates Foundation is pure Buffett. "... rational, original, breaking the mold of how extremely rich people donate money" is how Loomis describes it in "Warren Buffett Gives It Away." Buffett said he decided to make the gift to the Gates Foundation when he "came to realize that there was a terrific foundation that was already scaled-up—that wouldn't have to go through the real grind of getting to a megasize like the Buffett Foundation would—and that could productively use my money now." Buffett also attributed his decision to getting to know Bill and Melinda Gates well and growing to admire what they were doing with their foundation.

Buffett has pledged to gradually donate 85% of his Berkshire Hathaway stock to five foundations. Five-sixths of the shares will go to the Gates Foundation. The Gates Foundation is recognized for its pioneering work relating to improving world health, reducing extreme poverty and, in the United States, expanding educational opportunities and access to information technology.

Like Buffett's gift to the Bill & Melinda Gates Foundation, the Giving Pledge is an excellent example of big thinking because of its potential to expand the thinking of billionaires about how much of their wealth to give to charity. Under the Giving Pledge, the wealthiest people are encouraged to pledge at least 50% of their net worth to charity during their lifetimes or at death. In "The $600 Billion Challenge," Loomis describes the Giving Pledge as having "the potential to dramatically change the philanthropic behavior of Americans."

Loomis notes that as of September 2012, there were 92 signers of the Giving Pledge. The success of the Giving Pledge demonstrates the power of a big idea acted upon.[44]

There are many opportunities to apply original thinking to philanthropy and other worthwhile pursuits. The Giving Pledge and Buffett's gift of Berkshire Hathaway stock to the Bill & Melinda Gates Foundation are two excellent examples of big, original thinking. In the spirit of the Giving Pledge, I would like to challenge readers of this newsletter to volunteer

---

[44] For more information about the Giving Pledge, see: www.givingpledge.org.

time during the coming year applying their unique personal talents to an important charitable cause or issue. Knowing the talents of many of this newsletter's readers, such a gesture could have significance.

Warren Buffett on the Importance of a Well Chosen Circle of Friends

It is said that we are shaped by the company we keep. One theme that appears repeatedly in Loomis' book is the number and the quality of the friendships Buffett has. Throughout the book we read about Buffett meeting someone and becoming good friends.

The way Buffett thinks about investing has been strongly influenced by his mentor Benjamin Graham. In addition to Graham, Buffett has learned from and been influenced by a number of thoughtful, insightful, highly successful people, including, among many others, Tom Murphy, Louis Simpson, Ajit Jain, Don Graham, William Ruane, Walter Scott and Bill Gates. The breadth and depth of Buffett's relationships and his people skills are an important, perhaps under-appreciated aspect of his management skill and overall success. "He is the best judge of human talent there is," says Rich Santulli in Andy Serwer's article "The Oracle of Everything."

One friendship of particular note is Buffett's relationship with Charlie Munger. Buffett met Munger, an attorney also originally from Omaha, when both men were relatively early in their careers. Their business relationship grew over the years. As Loomis notes in "The Inside Story on Warren Buffett," Munger helped Buffett's value-orientated investment philosophy evolve. He "nudged, prodded and shoved" Buffett toward appreciating that he should pay reasonable, fair prices for good businesses, and did not have to buy only underpriced businesses. In addition to Munger, a number of other people with ties to Nebraska also contribute to the success of Berkshire Hathaway.

For additional commentary on Buffett's business philosophy, please see Edition #4 (board priorities, fiduciary duty) and Edition #5 (risk management, culture) of my newsletter.

QUESTIONS AND ANSWERS WITH CAROL LOOMIS

Carol Loomis, the distinguished editor and reporter for **Fortune**, has graciously agreed to discuss her book and provide additional insight on Warren Buffett and Berkshire Hathaway. Loomis is a close friend of Buffett's and has written a number of articles about him. It is rare that an author knows the person about whom she writes so well.

In the preface to the article "What Warren Thinks ..." you write that Warren Buffett the teacher is "the role for which he has said he would most like to be remembered." Please tell us more about this.

Ben Graham, Warren Buffett's mentor, also wished to be remembered as a teacher (and certainly Warren remembers him that way). Warren has taught with his writing and speeches in several ways: in his annual letter to shareholders (and in the Berkshire owners' manual), in which he has often branched out into essays, about such matters as derivatives and transaction costs; in Fortune articles he has written—e.g., the 1977 piece about inflation—and in his rare speeches, two of which Fortune turned into articles; in op-ed pieces, including the one about taxes that ran in the NYT last week; in his sessions with business students, as described in the very article you mention ("What Warren Thinks ...") and, for example, in "The Bill and Warren Show." *Tap Dancing to Work* is loaded with examples of his teaching.

Berkshire Hathaway's annual chairman's letter, which you have been editing since 1977, is one of the most eagerly anticipated pieces of corporate writing every year. What would you like to see more CEOs and corporations do with their annual letters?

The key to the quality of Warren's letter—and a very few others, such as Jamie Dimon's and Bob Wilmers' (he's the chairman of MTB)—is that they sit down and write their letters themselves, trying to give an honest picture of how their corporations fared during the past year. Most CEOs turn this job over to their public relations or investor relations people and what comes through is a weak, uninteresting missive. Now, I don't mean that what the CEO writes cannot be edited—writers always need editing. It's just that what needs to emerge from the process is the CEO's thinking, not the watered-down opinions of someone else.

You include in your book a memorable article on Warren Buffett entitled "The Best Advice I Ever Got." What is the best advice you ever got?

I'll mention two points: First, if you get a job offer from a company you like and respect, take it—without any thought about your pay. Any company you respect is apt to be a meritocracy, and if you're good you will do well in a meritocracy. Second, find out what time your boss gets in and get in earlier.

What is it like to play bridge with Warren Buffett?

He's a little better than I am, so I'm always trying to raise my game when I'm playing with him. He *is* capable of making a mistake now and then, and he berates himself when he does.

Thank you Carol.

THE ASSET WARREN BUFFETT VALUES MOST

Perhaps it is fitting that one of the last articles in Loomis' excellent book is about the asset Warren Buffett values most. In a book that focuses primarily on investment and business success, the asset most valued, interestingly, is not what one might expect.

In an article written by Buffett, "My Philanthropic Pledge," Buffett describes his motivation for committing to gradually give away all of his Berkshire Hathaway stock to philanthropic foundations. Buffett writes that his reaction to his "extraordinary good fortune" is not one of guilt, but rather of gratitude. While his charitable giving will be among the largest ever, he observes that many people make important contributions every single day in terms of their time and talent. Thus, Buffett concludes, reality sets "an obvious course" for his philosophy toward philanthropy. "Keep all we can conceivably need and distribute the rest to society, for its needs."

And the asset Buffett values most?

"The asset I most value, aside from health, is interesting, diverse, and long-standing friends."

WARREN BUFFETT'S ANNUAL LETTER TO SHAREHOLDERS OF BERKSHIRE HATHAWAY

Taking Fellow CEOs to Task: "Opportunities Abound in America" • Investing in Regulated, Capital-Intensive Industries

BILL GATES' ANNUAL LETTER FOR THE BILL & MELINDA GATES FOUNDATION

Why Annual Letters Are Important

In this edition of my newsletter, I highlight several important points Warren Buffett makes in his recent annual letter to shareholders of Berkshire Hathaway and discuss how they illustrate broader principles with respect to investing, law, regulation and business. Buffett's observations about investment opportunities for CEOs are especially noteworthy this year. Then I discuss Bill Gates' recent annual letter for the Bill & Melinda Gates Foundation and the insight it provides on the value of annual letters for both non-profit organizations and corporations.

WARREN BUFFETT'S ANNUAL LETTER: "AMERICA'S DESTINY ... EVER-INCREASING ABUNDANCE"

Warren Buffett's annual letters are known for being informative and thought provoking. In his most recent annual letter,[45] I found especially

---

[45] Warren Buffett's annual letter to shareholders of Berkshire Hathaway for the year 2012 is available at: http://www.berkshirehathaway.com/letters/2012ltr.pdf. The complete 2012 Berkshire Hathaway annual report is available at: http://www.berkshirehathaway.com/2012ar/2012ar.pdf.

interesting Buffett's comments on investment opportunities and the hesitation of some of his fellow CEOs to invest.

Buffett took CEOs to task for not being more decisive about investing in their companies. "There was a lot of hand-wringing last year among CEOs who cried 'uncertainty' when faced with capital-allocation decisions (despite many of their businesses having enjoyed record levels of both earnings and cash). At Berkshire, we didn't share their fears ..."

In 2012 Berkshire Hathaway spent a record $9.8 billion on plant and equipment, most of it in the United States. This was 19% more than in 2011, the previous high. Buffett expects Berkshire Hathaway to have another record year for capital expenditures in 2013. Buffett also said Berkshire Hathaway would continue to seek out large acquisitions similar to the recent $28 billion H.J. Heinz deal.

Buffett wrote that his optimism is based on his belief that American business and stocks, whose fate is tied to business performance, "will do fine over time ... Periodic setbacks will occur, yes, but investors and managers are in a game that is heavily stacked in their favor ...

> ... Since the game is so favorable, Charlie [Munger] and I believe it's a terrible mistake to try to dance in and out of it based upon the turn of tarot cards, the predictions of 'experts,' or the ebb and flow of business activity. The risks of being out of the game are huge compared to the risks of being in it.

Given Buffett's track record (and given how broad a proportion of the U.S. economy Berkshire Hathaway now represents), perhaps more CEOs should be taking note and investing more in their businesses.

"We will keep our foot to the floor ... Opportunities abound in America."

Investing in Regulated, Capital-Intensive Industries

Government policy plays an important role in encouraging certain types of investments. Buffett's comments on investing in regulated, capital-intensive industries highlight a second important issue in his annual letter.

Buffett provides instructive insight into how government policy influences capital investment in his discussion of two major Berkshire Hathaway operations, the railroad operator BNSF and the electric utility MidAmerican Energy. Both operations are huge. Buffett notes that BNSF carries about 15% of all inter-city freight in America, more ton-miles of goods than any other company. The electric utilities of MidAmerican serve retail customers in 10 states. Only one utility holding company serves more states than MidAmerican. Both operations require huge amounts of investment in very long-lived, regulated assets.

Buffett writes that he and his managers "relish" making huge capital investments if they promise reasonable returns. To make such large capital commitments, Buffett notes that he and his managers must "put a large amount of trust in future regulation." Given the significance of future regulation, it is easy to appreciate the importance of in-depth knowledge of government policy (and how it could change in the future) for successful investing in regulated industries.

Buffett's investment decisions with respect to regulated, capital-intensive companies like BNSF and MidAmerican Energy are informed by a nuanced understanding of the legal and regulatory environment in which the companies operate. His investment process is an excellent example of how quality legal and regulatory insight and analysis add real value to investment decision making.[46]

Additional Highlights

In addition to the investment and regulatory themes discussed above, Buffett also discusses corporate performance, acquisitions, four disciplines supporting his insurance operations and a variety of other topics in his annual letter. Buffett devotes three pages to explaining Berkshire Hathaway's divided policy. Buffett's independent, analytical thought process is on display in his discussion of how his opinion has evolved about buying selected newspapers.

---

[46] Banking and insurance, two additional highly-regulated industries in which Buffett invests, are also examples of industries where knowledge of their legal and regulatory environment is essential for investment and business success. As discussed in earlier Editions of this newsletter, regulatory reform is changing the business of banking in significant ways.

Buffett did not mention succession. But, like in earlier annual letters, he did laud a number of people considered potential successors. Tony Nicely, Ajit Jain, Tad Montross, Matt Rose, Greg Abel and others received words of praise. "Todd Combs and Ted Weschler, our new investment managers, have proved to be smart, models of integrity, helpful to Berkshire in many ways beyond portfolio management, and a perfect cultural fit," Buffett noted. "We hit the jackpot with these two."

Buffett's people skills are an important part of his success. The importance of hiring and working with people with intelligence, integrity and common sense cannot be over-emphasized.

––––––––––––––––––

Buffett's annual letters are available at the Berkshire Hathaway website.[47] I highly recommend reading them. For additional commentary on Buffett's business philosophy and annual letters to shareholders, please see Edition #8 of my newsletter.

The Berkshire Hathaway annual meeting is May 4 in Omaha. I will be attending. If you will be in Omaha and would like to meet for coffee, please let me know.

BILL GATES' ANNUAL LETTER FOR THE BILL & MELINDA GATES FOUNDATION

Why Annual Letters Are Important

After Warren Buffett made his multi-billion dollar pledge to the Bill & Melinda Gates Foundation, which effectively doubled the resources of the foundation, he encouraged Bill Gates to follow his example and write an annual letter. Commenting on this in his first annual letter for the Gates Foundation,[48] Gates wrote that "I won't be quoting Mae West or trying to match his humor, but I will try to be equally candid." He went on to add:

––––––––––––––––––

[47] Warren Buffett's annual letters to shareholders of Berkshire Hathaway for the years 1977-2012 are available at:
http://www.berkshirehathaway.com/letters/letters.html.
[48] Bill Gates' 2009 annual letter for the Bill & Melinda Gates Foundation is available at: http://www.gatesfoundation.org/Who-We-Are/Resources-and-Media/Annual-Letters-List/Annual-Letter-2009.

> In this letter I want to share in a frank way what our goals are and where progress is being made and where it is not.

What Gates had to say about his first annual letter is a pretty good summary of how CEOs of many types of organizations should think about annual letters. The purpose of an annual letter is to inform and educate stakeholders about the goals, objectives, mission and progress of an organization. The best annual letters also give readers an honest picture of the CEO's thinking.

In Gates' most recent annual letter,[49] he writes about the importance of "using a tool of business [accurate measurement] to improve the health and welfare of more of the world's people." The goals that Gates writes about – eradicating polio, reducing hunger and poverty, improving the quality of education – are challenging. But progress is being made. "... I have been struck again and again by how important measurement is to improving the human condition. You can achieve amazing progress if you set a clear goal and find a measure that will drive progress toward that goal ..."

Buffett and Gates both write at length about performance measurement and about goals and objectives in their annual letters. In Buffett's annual letters, he writes about Berkshire Hathaway's operating results, major acquisitions and performance goals and objectives,[50] as well as broader themes, including accounting, valuation, stock options, board responsibilities, shareholder rights and Berkshire Hathaway's acquisition philosophy. In Gates' most recent annual letter, he discusses at length how performance measurement helps foundations and government programs determine whether and how their goals are being achieved.

For CEOs more generally, writing an annual letter themselves (rather than turning the project over to the public relations or investor relations

---

[49] Bill Gates' 2013 annual letter for the Bill & Melinda Gates Foundation is available at: http://www.gatesfoundation.org/Who-We-Are/Resources-and-Media/Annual-Letters-List/Annual-Letter-2013.

[50] More specifically, in describing the performance "yardstick" he and Vice Chairman Charlie Munger use, Buffett writes in his 2012 annual letter: "It's our *job* to increase intrinsic business value – for which we use book value as a *significantly understated* proxy -- at a faster rate than the market gains of the S&P." For additional insight on Berkshire Hathaway's performance objectives, see the 2012 annual letter.

department) is important for variety of reasons. Writing an annual letter personally allows a CEO to communicate directly with donors, shareholders, analysts and other key stakeholders. Writing an annual letter personally helps the CEO give key stakeholders a better sense of the person leading the organization, which can help build stakeholder trust and "buy in" to the mission of the organization. Writing an annual letter personally is also important because, by so doing, a CEO demonstrates that he or she has thought through the goals and objectives of the organization and the means by which to achieve them.

To accomplish ambitious goals in philanthropy, business and other endeavors in life, it is important to articulate a clear vision and to engage others. Writing a well-thought-through annual letter is an excellent way to do both.

Gates' annual letters are available at the Bill & Melinda Gates Foundation website.[51] I highly recommend reading them.

------

[51] Bill Gates' annual letters for the Bill & Melinda Gates Foundation for the years 2009-2013 are available at: http://www.gatesfoundation.org/Who-We-Are/Resources-and-Media/Annual-Letters-List.

PAUL VOLCKER ESTABLISHES THE VOLCKER ALLIANCE TO STRENGTHEN TRUST IN GOVERNMENT

The Example of Cities

THE U.S. FEDERAL RESERVE PREPARES NEW RULES FOR FOREIGN BANKING ORGANIZATIONS

New Capital and Liquidity Requirements • Implications for Future International Cooperation on Regulation?

In this edition of my newsletter, I discuss the establishment of the new Volcker Alliance. Paul Volcker, perhaps best known for fighting inflation as Chairman of the Federal Reserve during the Carter and Reagan Administrations, recently established the nonpartisan Volcker Alliance to strengthen public trust in basic government services. Then I discuss new rules that the U.S. Federal Reserve is preparing for foreign banking organizations with U.S. operations and the broader implications of the new rules for foreign banks and for international banking regulation.

THE VOLCKER ALLIANCE

Former Federal Reserve Chairman Paul Volcker, most recently known for his efforts to promote financial regulatory reform and the eponymous Volcker Rule, established the Volcker Alliance to improve how government works at the city, state and federal level. The mission of the Volcker Alliance is to improve the execution of public policy and rebuild public trust in government.

Volcker has said that trust in governments in the U.S. and other democracies has been declining for decades. Volcker has attributed this lack of trust to an inability of governments to respond effectively to the challenges of the day in the eyes of their citizens.

The Volcker Alliance will sponsor research on government performance, make recommendations for policy development and implementation, and provide a forum for discussion of new ideas and tools to strengthen policy execution at all levels of government. Shelley Metzenbaum will be the president of the Volcker Alliance. Board members will include William Donaldson, former Chairman of the Securities and Exchange Commission, and Alice Rivlin, former Vice Chairman of the Federal Reserve.

Volcker has pointed to the implementation of the **Volcker Rule** as one example of government ineffectiveness. The Volcker Rule generally prohibits banks from engaging in short-term proprietary trading for their own account. The Volcker Rule was approved as part of the Dodd-Frank Wall Street Reform and Consumer Protection Act, which was signed into law in July 2010. The rules implementing the Volcker Rule have yet to be finalized, as five federal regulatory agencies continue to work out details of the rule. About two-thirds of Dodd-Frank's rulemaking deadlines have been missed as its third anniversary approaches.

While there are numerous think tanks, universities and other organizations writing papers on policy and governance, Volcker hopes to distinguish the work of the Volcker Alliance by focusing on the practical nuts and bolts of governance rather than on theory. One example of this practical approach will be exploring ways to promote the training of bank examiners who might be given the task of enforcing the Volcker Rule and other complex new financial rules and regulations.

Given its focus on the practical, the Volcker Alliance (and other organizations addressing similar issues) might be wise to look at the example of certain cities, like New York, London and Singapore, where an emphasis of practical solutions has led to some noteworthy results in recent years.[52] Some cities have found constructive and creative ways to bring

---

[52] It is noteworthy to consider, for example, what Singapore has accomplished in health care and education and what New York and London have done recently to improve the quality of life in big cities.

diverse interest groups together to work on issues of common concern. Some cities have also benefited from bringing in leadership and ideas from the private sector.

THE U.S. FEDERAL RESERVE PREPARES NEW RULES FOR FOREIGN BANKING ORGANIZATIONS

New Capital and Liquidity Requirements

Implications for Future International Cooperation on Regulation?

Following a lengthy public comment process, the U.S. Federal Reserve is currently working on finalizing far-reaching new rules for foreign banking organizations with U.S. operations.[53] As proposed, the new rules would require foreign banking organizations with a significant U.S. presence to create an intermediate holding company over their U.S. subsidiaries. Foreign banks would also be required to maintain stronger capital and liquidity positions in the U.S.

The proposed rules generally apply to foreign banking organizations with a U.S. banking presence and total global consolidated assets of $50 billion or more. A foreign banking organization with both $50 billion or more in global consolidated assets and U.S. subsidiaries with $10 billion or more in total assets generally would be required to organize its U.S. subsidiaries under an intermediate holding company. The proposed rules would implement enhanced prudential standards and early remediation requirements set out in the Dodd-Frank Wall Street Reform and Consumer Protection Act.

If implemented as proposed, the new rules would mark the beginning of a new era of regulation and supervision for foreign banking organizations in the U.S. Regulation of foreign banks in the U.S. has changed relatively little in the past decade, in spite of the rapid expansion of some foreign banks' U.S. operations from traditional lending to large, complex trading and capital markets activities. The proposed rules are also intended to

---

[53] Board of Governors of the Federal Reserve System, Proposed Rule, "Enhanced Prudential Standards and Early Remediation Requirements for Foreign Banking Organizations and Foreign Nonbank Financial Companies" (December 17, 2012). Available at:
http://www.federalreserve.gov/newsevents/press/bcreg/bcreg20121214a.pdf.

address issues relating to the risks that large, interconnected financial institutions pose to U.S. financial stability.

Banking regulators in countries outside the U.S. have expressed reservations about the proposed rules. Germany's Bundesbank and Bafin stated in an April 26 letter to the Federal Reserve that "'go it alone' national initiatives can tend to weaken the global setup and stability" of global systemically important banks "instead of stabilizing them."[54] They also stated that the proposed rules put coordinated supervision of internationally active banks at risk and represent a tendency toward "'renationalizing' supervision, which, in fact, harbors real potential for supervisory arbitrage and global imbalances." Concerns have also been raised that the proposed rules could affect future negotiations with non-U.S. jurisdictions and regulators regarding liberalizing cross-border financial services.

In spite of the opposition, Federal Reserve officials have indicated that they are unlikely to back down over the proposed rules because during the financial crisis some of the biggest borrowers from their emergency facilities were foreign banking groups. "Many large foreign banking organizations came to rely heavily on short-term, wholesale U.S. dollar funding and thereby became subject to destabilizing runs," said Federal Reserve Governor Daniel K. Tarullo, at the time the proposed rules were announced.[55]

For foreign banks subject to the proposed rules, complying with the new requirements would require a significant amount of implementation work. For many foreign banks, the proposed rules would require significant restructuring, additional capital, [56] changes to business lines, operational

---

[54] The letter from the Bundesbank and Bafin is available at: http://www.federalreserve.gov/SECRS/2013/April/20130426/R-1438/R-1438_042613_111089_571489255536_1.pdf.

[55] Federal Reserve Governor Daniel K.Tarullo's statement is available at: http://www.federalreserve.gov/newsevents/press/bcreg/tarullo20121214a.htm.

[56] The proposed rules could lead to significant internal transfers of capital within some large foreign banks and could require some banks to raise significant amounts of additional capital. See Jesse Hamilton, Bloomberg, "Deutsche Bank Warns of Failures Under Proposed U.S. Rules (May 1, 2013). Available at: http://www.bloomberg.com/news/2013-05-01/deutsche-bank-warns-of-failures-under-proposed-u-s-rules.html.

changes and additional compliance.[57] The Federal Reserve has estimated that more than two dozen foreign banking organizations would be required to establish intermediate holding companies.

The Federal Reserve received a large number of comments from foreign regulators, financial institutions and the public on the proposed rules. The Federal Reserve is working to issue its final rules for foreign banking organizations before the end of the year. The final rules may contain some concessions for foreign banking organizations with a relatively small U.S. presence. As the rules are currently written, foreign banking organizations with global consolidated assets of $50 billion or more on July 1, 2014, would be required to meet the new standards on July 1, 2015.

---

[57] Given the size, scope and complexity of the proposed rules, senior executives and board members would be well advised to begin familiarizing themselves with the proposed rules and their implications early in order to plan ahead most effectively.

CHINA UNVEILS BASIC PLAN FOR
SHANGHAI FREE TRADE ZONE

Potentially the Most Significant Economic Development in China in Years • Opportunities Created by the Free Trade Zone

QUESTIONS AND ANSWERS WITH MARK DUVAL OF AMCHAM CHINA ABOUT DOING BUSINESS IN CHINA

In this edition of my newsletter, I discuss the recently launched Shanghai Free Trade Zone (the SHFTZ). The creation of the SHFTZ is potentially a very important development with respect to the future shape of China's economic policy. The policy documents that have been made public provide insight into government thinking about how China's economy could develop. Then, in a Question and Answer, Mark Duval, President of the American Chamber of Commerce in the People's Republic of China, shares his thoughts about doing business in China. The SHFTZ "may well be the third most important milestone in China's modern economic reform story," he observes.

THE SHANGHAI FREE TRADE ZONE

China Launches the Shanghai Free Trade Zone

On September 29, China launched its much-anticipated China (Shanghai) Pilot Free Trade Zone. The significance of the SHFTZ could be comparable to that of the Shenzhen Special Economic Zone (the Shenzhen SEZ), which was established more than 30 years ago, in that it could serve as China's testing ground for broader economic reforms. The Shenzhen

SEZ policy reform focused on manufacturing and led to a sustained period of significant economic growth. The new SHFTZ policy reform concentrates primarily on services and financial reform. The initial size of the SHFTZ is relatively small (about 29 square kilometers).[58] If the economic reforms underlying the SHFTZ are successful and subsequently adopted across China, they could lead to a new wave of liberalization that could have a fundamental impact on China's larger economy.

In spite of the hype surrounding the launch of the SHFTZ, the official launch itself was relatively subdued. Few senior government officials showed up. Prime Minister Li Keqiang has personally championed the free trade zone.

Why the Shanghai Free Trade Zone is Significant

The policy reforms underlying the SHFTZ are comprehensive and far-reaching in nature. In some areas of policy reform (such as business service sector liberalization), it is relatively clear how the SHFTZ policies will seek to liberalize markets. In others areas (such as financial reforms), the policy reforms are less specific and so the scope of these reforms is more of an open question.

As described in more detail below, the SHFTZ policy reforms impact many areas of business, finance and administration. Some of the major areas of liberalization and reform include:

- Further opening many business service sectors to foreign investors and reforming the manner in which foreign investment is administered;
- Encouraging multinational companies to establish regional headquarters and operations centers with trading and logistics functions in the SHFTZ; and

---

[58] At its launch, the Shanghai Free Trade Zone will cover a non-contiguous area of about 29 square kilometers in Shanghai's Pudong New Area. The free trade zone will consist of four existing bonded zones: the Waigaoqiao Free Trade Zone, the Waigaoqiao Free Trade Logistics Park, the Yangshan Free Trade Port Area and the Pudong Airport Comprehensive Free Trade Zone. The free trade zone may eventually be expanded to cover the entire Pudong district in Shanghai, which covers about 1,210 square kilometers.

- Under the precondition that risks can be controlled, creating conditions to test Yuan convertibility, market based interest rates and cross border use of the Chinese currency.

One objective of the SHFTZ is to give Shanghai municipal government officials the opportunity to experiment with significant reforms inside a controlled free trade zone. Policies that are deemed effective could then be rolled out across China.

While the SHFTZ is called a "free trade zone," the policy reform underlying the SHFTZ is meant to be much broader than what is typically associated with a free trade zone and to include helping create a more open and dynamic economy and helping make China's business service sectors more competitive globally. The SHFTZ opens up new business opportunities in a wide variety of areas.[59]

Policy Measures Underlying the Shanghai Free Trade Zone

The launching of the SHFTZ represents a coordinated effort among policymakers at many levels of government in China. The State Council, the chief administrative authority of China, issued the *Overall Plan for the China (Shanghai) Pilot Free Trade Zone* (the Overall Plan), on September 27. The Overall Plan is the overarching policy framework for economic liberalization within the free trade zone. Two days later, on September 29, the Shanghai municipal government issued the *Special Administrative Measures on the Entry of Foreign Investment into the China (Shanghai) Pilot Free Trade Zone* (2013 Negative List) (the Negative List) and additional measures for the administration of the SHFTZ. (The significance of the Negative List is discussed below.)

A number of additional policymaking bodies have also approved measures to help facilitate the SHFTZ. The Standing Committee of the National People's Congress, the top legislative authority, issued a decision to help streamline the process of setting up enterprises in the free trade zone. A

---

[59] It is worth noting that the Overall Plan includes a general policy statement that enterprises established within the SHFTZ "in principle" will not be subject to geographical operating limits within China and may invest and conduct business outside of the free trade zone. While this general policy statement has not yet been included in more specific pronouncements, it does merit monitoring and could have significant implications for doing business in China in the future.

number of additional industry regulators and agencies, including the Ministry of Finance, the People's Bank of China, the General Administration of Customs, the China Banking Regulatory Commission, the China Securities Regulatory Commission and the State Administration of Foreign Exchange, have also issued measures relating to the SHFTZ.

Given the far-reaching nature of the objectives of the SHFTZ, it will take the cooperation of many parts and levels of government in China to make the economic liberalization goals underlying the SHFTZ a success.

The Negative List

The Overall Plan provides that a "negative list" approach will be used toward foreign investment in the SHFTZ. Under a negative list approach, national treatment will generally be given to foreign investment in business sectors that are not listed as prohibited or restricted in the new Negative List. The Negative List was published by the Shanghai municipal government on October 1.

The negative list approach represents a significant step forward for foreign investments. Prior to the establishment of the Negative List, foreign investments were generally subject to an approval process by the Ministry of Commerce and its local counterparts. Now, if a foreign investment is not listed on the Negative List, the enterprise or project generally only needs to complete a record filing process with the Shanghai municipal government.

Within the SHFTZ, the Negative List effectively replaces the *Foreign Investment Industrial Guidance Catalogue*. The catalogue sets out business sectors in which foreign investment is encouraged, restricted or prohibited in China.

The Negative List will be updated from time to time to reflect the evolving development and investment needs of the free trade zone.

Financial Reform

Details have been relatively light about the shape of financial reform policies underlying the SHFTZ. The Overall Plan states that "under the precondition that risks can be controlled," China will create conditions in the free trade zone to test Yuan convertibility, market based interest rates and the cross border use of the Chinese currency. Other government guidance on financial reform has been light. Given the fundamental nature of financial reform, the manner in which specific financial reforms are unveiled in the free trade zone will probably be gradual and incremental.

The shape of financial reform is worth watching closely. Financial reform is a key element of the trial liberalizations contemplated under the SHFTZ. One of China's goals is to transform Shanghai into an international financial center similar to Hong Kong by 2020.

Service Sector Liberalization

The Overall Plan includes measures to provide equal market access to foreign investors in six investment areas (consisting of 18 business service sectors). The Overall Plan removes market entry restrictions and certain foreign investor qualification requirements for these areas of business. The investment areas and service sectors subject to liberalization include the following:

- Financial Services (banking, specialized health and medical insurance and leasing services);
- Shipping Services (ocean shipping and international vessel management);
- Trade and Commercial Services (value-added telecommunications services and the sales and service of entertainment and game consoles);
- Professional Services (legal services, credit investigations, travel agencies, investment management, engineering design and construction services);
- Cultural Services (entertainment venues); and
- Social Services (educational and vocational training and medical services).

Some business service sector liberalizations reflect changes that are already underway in certain parts of China's economy. For example, significant infrastructure investments have been made by China's central government and the Shanghai government in recent years to help establish Shanghai as a leading shipping center. The shipping services liberalizations included in the SHFTZ policies should help expand this effort.

Expediting Imports

An additional objective of the SHFTZ is to simplify and expedite the process of importing goods into China. Currently, it can take up to a month for goods to clear customs. Speeding up imports would allow supply chains to operate more efficiently.

For additional information about how policy reforms affect specific areas of business and create business opportunities, please contact me.

The Shanghai Free Trade Zone and China's Bigger Picture

As noted in the introduction, the launch of the Shanghai Free Trade Zone has been compared to the launch of the Shenzhen Special Economic Zone. More than 30 years ago, China launched the Shenzhen SEZ near Hong Kong to experiment with broad economic reforms. Over a period of time, policy changes were tested before being rolled out across China. Policies that were developed contributed to a sustained period of economic growth and China became globally competitive in manufacturing.

With the launch of the SHFTZ, China has begun a new period of experimenting with economic liberalization. This time the reform efforts focus primarily on financial reform and the services component of China's economy. In some areas of reform (such as policies relating to the liberalization of certain specific business service sectors) it is relatively clear how the policies underlying the SHFTZ will seek to liberalize markets. In other areas of reform (including reforms relating to Yuan convertibility, market based interest rates and tax reform), the shape of reform is less specific and so the scope and timing of these reforms is more of an open question. The manner in which fundamental reforms are unveiled will probably be gradual and measured.

The recent announcements about the SHFTZ should be viewed in the larger context of economic policymaking in China. The SHFTZ is one of several current initiatives, including investment and trade talks, to make China's economy more competitive and to encourage economic development. Additional insight about the future shape of China's economic policymaking may emerge from the upcoming Third Plenary Session of the 18th Central Committee of the Communist Party of China.

As Mark Duval of AmCham China points out in the Question and Answer following, China's leadership does understand that significant economic reforms are necessary. Important questions now include what the specific details about the economic liberalizations will be and when the reforms will occur. The policy underlying the Shanghai Free Trade Zone provides significant insight into these important questions about China's bigger picture.

QUESTIONS AND ANSWERS WITH MARK DUVAL

Mark Duval, President of the American Chamber of Commerce in the People's Republic of China (AmCham China), has graciously agreed to discuss the business and political environment in China. Duval oversees the general administration of AmCham China, a nonprofit organization which represents U.S. companies and individuals doing business in China. More than 3,500 individuals from more than 1,000 companies are members of AmCham China. The headquarters of AmCham China are in Beijing.

China's State Council recently approved the creation of and announced rules for a pilot free trade zone for Shanghai. While details are still to come, the action may allow, among other things, freer Yuan convertibility, the liberalization of interest rates and the relaxation of restrictions on foreign investment. What are the most significant opportunities you see arising from the new free trade zone? What does this development represent for China's future financial and trade liberalization more generally?

This may well be the third most important milestone in China's modern economic reform story.

After 30 years of blistering growth, the current Chinese economic model is approaching breaking point, with severe strains manifesting in ways well explored by the international media. I'm mostly convinced the new leadership fully understands – possibly even more urgently than external observers do – that the current economic structure has to shift dramatically, and that the country has to move away from dependence on investment and exports to a more market oriented, self-sustaining, significantly less capital intensive model – with service sector and financial liberalization at the core.

However, beneficiaries of the current system are many and resistant, making rapid change inconceivably difficult. The SHFTZ is a dramatic thrust against these resistant forces and towards economic change and represents an historic opportunity for future financial, trade and investment liberalization.

What differences do you see with respect to U.S. companies' businesses and operations in China since the Xi Jinping Administration came to power?

Leadership change brings uncertainty and anxiety, and in this particular case U.S. companies in China are both anxious and hopeful.

Anxious due to the unpredictable, opaque, and often heavy handed ways the new government is pursuing its current agenda. For example, the current crackdown on corruption in business – welcome as such an initiative is – appears to focus on certain sectors and participants and ignores others with shifting rationale and occasional nationalistic fervor.

In this unpredictable political environment US companies feel threatened yet remain hopeful due to the frequent signals from Beijing that dramatic market oriented reforms in the service sector, agricultural markets and overall investment environment are imminent.

With the cost of labor rising in China, low-cost labor and exports will probably play a less central role in China's future economic growth and development. What policy changes (e.g., with respect to foreign investment, transparency, standards and/or intellectual property rights) should China make in order to foster a more productive and innovative workforce and economy?

The SHFTZ stated ambitions are an excellent proxy for the national policy changes required to drive China's future economic growth and development, however policy change is only a part of the equation. Fundamental deep-rooted hurdles remain in the areas of systemic corruption and the challenges associated with consistent nationwide enforcement of laws and regulations. In my view this will be the ultimate challenge for overcoming the middle income trap and realizing sustained long term economic growth in China.

Environmental issues are an ongoing concern in China. What opportunities are there for U.S. companies to help address air quality issues in China? Water quality issues? Other environmental issues?

Addressing environmental issues is high on the agenda of the Xi Administration particularly in areas most visible to the public, so air and water related environmental technologies will have the greater opportunities - specifically, large scale upstream industrial technologies. On the consumer side, household oriented filtration and cleansing solutions will find rapidly growing markets.

The success of high-speed inter-city passenger rail service in China has exceeded the expectations of many people. Prime Minister Li Keqiang recently said that China would invest $100 billion a year in its train system for years to come, mainly on high-speed rail. What opportunities does the continuing development of high-speed rail create for U.S. companies doing business in China? How is the increasing availability of high-speed transportation in China affecting how business is conducted in China?

Infrastructure and system providers currently enjoying the build out of the passenger rail system in China will continue to benefit from continued strong growth but the real story is how high speed interconnectivity is transforming the horizontality of China. As a phenomenon it's still early in development but the increasing high speed mobility of businesspeople across the country will accelerate overall service sector development and particularly fuel the growth of national consumer product brands – particularly benefiting local and regional Chinese companies.

Companies that cater to China's rapidly growing middle class, including fast food chains and a wide variety of retail brands, are finding success in China. What advice do you have for companies wishing to build a presence and increase consumer-orientated sales in China?

American retail and consumer brands are highly valued by China's middle class – the opportunities are endless and growing. Invest carefully but invest now.

Six large U.S. and U.K. hedge fund organizations are set to receive regulatory approval to raise money from institutions within China for investing overseas. The hedge funds are expected to be permitted to raise about $50 million each under the pilot Qualified Domestic Limited Partner program. The move is seen as a small but significant step in opening China's capital account and removing barriers separating China from international financial markets. What are the implications of this new policy? Do you expect Chinese regulators to continue their practice of making incremental changes to the regulation of financial markets and to broaden this program in the future?

I anticipate significant change in China's financial market environment over the next 18 months. The SHFTZ will be a leading indicator but other incremental reforms to open China's capital account, generally open the financial marketplace to foreign investors and accelerate the convertibility of the Yuan will play out steadily.

China's economic growth is backed by the "three carriages" (investment, export and consumption). How do you see U.S. companies supporting these three growth areas looking forward?

Existing participants in investment and exports arenas will continue to benefit from related growth but significantly, as Chinese service sector and consumer oriented growth accelerates as a share of GDP, the U.S. competitive advantage in these areas should provide accelerating opportunities for U.S. business.

The American Chamber of Commerce in the People's Republic of China has a membership of more than 3,500 individuals representing more than 1,000 companies. If you conducted a poll of AmCham China members about their expectations with respect to China's rate of economic growth, what would the results tell us?

We are about to launch our 2013 member survey. Results will be available on our website in early 2014. (The website for AmCham China is at www.amchamchina.org.)

In addition to the issues discussed above, what are the principal concerns of members of AmCham China with respect to doing business in China today?

Investing in China has great potential for U.S. business and there are many success stories, but it's still much more of a gamble than in many other parts of the world. In particular, the opaque and uneven enforcement of laws and regulations across the country significantly undermines the confidence of the business community.

Overall our members are looking for clear policy and consistent, transparent application of the rule of law, including allowing companies to legitimately defend themselves and their intellectual property. These fundamental prerequisites to building a fair and predictable business environment so that our businesses can invest, operate and expand with confidence remain elusive and continue to present the greatest challenge to sustainably do business in China.

Beijing is known for its restaurants. What are your favorite restaurants in Beijing?

It's true, Beijing has a phenomenal range of restaurants featuring cuisines from all over the world - my favorites however remain off-the-beaten-expat-path local venues offering spicy Sichuan, Hunan and Yunnan adventures.

What is your favorite thing to do on the weekend in Beijing?

With the recent birth of my second son I'm enjoying precious time with my family – but family and weather permitting you'll find me searching through the rough on one of Beijing's finest golf courses.

Thank you, Mark.

ENCOURAGING CHARITABLE ACTIVITY: THE UNITED STATES' EXPERIENCE

The Size and Scope of Nonprofit Activity in the United States • Charitable Policies and Practices in Other Countries • How Countries and Policymakers Can Encourage the Development of Nonprofit and Charitable Organizations

NONPROFIT ORGANIZATIONS AND A COUNTRY'S BIGGER PICTURE

The Nonprofit Sector: A New Source of Economic Dynamism

In this edition of my newsletter, I describe the United States' experience in encouraging charitable activity and then discuss how policymakers in other countries can promote the development of their own domestic nonprofit sectors. The size and scope of the nonprofit sector in the United States is larger than many people realize. Approximately $316.23 billion was donated to nonprofit organizations in the U.S. in 2012. Additionally, volunteers donate billions of hours of their time each year to nonprofit and charitable activities. The value of goods and services provided by U.S. nonprofit organizations was approximately 5.37% of gross domestic product in 2013.

A number of factors have contributed to the growth and development of the nonprofit sector and charitable activity in the United States. These factors include an underlying foundation of supportive laws and policies, tax incentives, culture, tradition and individual example. Many additional countries also have well-established nonprofit sectors and deeply-rooted charitable traditions. There are a variety of lessons that policymakers can learn from the experience of the United States and other countries with nonprofit organizations in order to help promote the development of dynamic, well-governed and accountable nonprofit sectors in their home countries.

Encouraging the development of a country's nonprofit sector can be valuable for a number of reasons. Nonprofit and charitable organizations provide social services that might otherwise need to be provided by the state. Nonprofits create jobs. By fostering the development of a robust, well-governed nonprofit sector, policymakers can help a country strengthen its legal and institutional framework, diversify its economy and develop an additional source of economic dynamism.

ENCOURAGING CHARITABLE ACTIVITY: THE UNITED STATES' EXPERIENCE

The Size and Scope of Nonprofit Activity in the United States; The Size of Donations and Volunteer Participation

The nonprofit sector is larger and plays a more dynamic role in the U.S. economy than many people realize. The U.S. recognizes a number of different types of nonprofit organizations. These include universities, hospitals, arts organizations, cultural organizations, youth sports programs and religious organizations. Nonprofit organizations provide a wide variety of goods and services, including food, health services, education, job training, child daycare and economic development services. The value of goods and services provided by U.S. nonprofit organizations was approximately 5.37% of gross domestic product in 2013.[60]

Nonprofit organizations receive their funding through fees, private donations, government grants, investment income and other sources. Approximately $316.23 billion was donated to nonprofit and charitable organizations in 2012, of which $228.93 billion was from individuals, $45.74 billion was from foundations, $23.41 billion was from bequests and $18.15 billion was from corporations. Additionally, volunteers donated

---

[60] Based on data from the Bureau of Economic Analysis, U.S. Department of Commerce.

approximately 7.9 billion hours of their time to nonprofit and charitable organizations during 2011.[61] In 2011, more than 64.3 million Americans worked as volunteers.[62]

The U.S. nonprofit sector has become an increasingly entrepreneurial and dynamic part of the U.S. economy. Nonprofits play a central role in many of the leading parts of the U.S. economy, including higher education, health care and basic scientific research. Proportionately, the nonprofit sector grew faster from 2000-2010 in terms of employees and wages in the U.S. than either business or government.[63]

Factors Underlying the Development of Nonprofit and Charitable Organizations

A number of factors have contributed to the growth and success of the nonprofit sector and charitable activity in the United States. Part of this growth and development can be attributed to laws, policies and institutions that federal, state and local governments have developed over time. Culture and individual involvement also play a very important role.

Factors that have played a fundamental role in the development of the nonprofit sector in the United States include:

- An underlying foundation of laws and policies;
- Tax policy and tax incentives;
- Culture and tradition; and
- Individual example and leadership.

Working together, these four factors have helped create an environment in which people are comfortable with giving their time and money to charitable causes and organizations. These factors have also helped create an environment in which nonprofits can thrive as individual organizations.

---

[61] Charitable donation data and volunteer data are from "Giving USA 2013: The Annual Report on Philanthropy for the Year 2012," researched and written by the Indiana University Lilly Family School of Philanthropy.

[62] Based on World Bank population data and Giving USA volunteer data.

[63] From The Nonprofit Almanac 2012, using estimates based on data from the Economic Census, the Bureau of Economic Analysis, the Bureau of Labor Statistics and the National Center for Charitable Statistics.

Each of these four factors is discussed in greater detail below.

Laws and Policies Underlying Nonprofit Organizations

Over the years, a legal and policy framework has been developed in the United States to encourage the establishment and growth of nonprofit and charitable organizations. At the foundation of this framework are laws and polices whose objectives are to encourage the development of transparent, well-governed and accountable organizations. Corporate law and tax law both play an important role in the regulation of nonprofit organizations. (Tax policy is discussed separately below.)

Most nonprofits are organized as corporations in the U.S. Being organized as a corporation requires a nonprofit to fulfill a number of ongoing financial, recordkeeping and corporate governance requirements. A board of directors is responsible for overseeing the management of a corporation. Directors are required to perform specific duties, including monitoring for potential conflicts of interest and exercising independent judgment for the overall benefit of the corporation. The corporate structure protects nonprofit staff and board members from being personally liable for actions of the corporate entity. Nonprofits are required to file tax returns and are subject to being audited. Nonprofits are also generally required to submit annual financial reports to the state in which they are incorporated.

The transparency of nonprofit organizations is enhanced through the work of organizations like GuideStar USA, Inc. GuideStar is a nonprofit that has created a database of information from the federal tax returns of nonprofit organizations and additional sources. Donors, grant makers, nonprofit leaders, government officials and others use GuideStar's website to find information about the programs, finances and impact of more than 1.8 million nonprofits recognized by the U.S. Internal Revenue Service.

Tax Policy and Tax Incentives

Tax policy and tax incentives are a second important part of the legal and policy framework that has been developed in the United States to encourage the growth and development of nonprofit organizations. The U.S. provides tax incentives to encourage individuals and corporations to make donations to nonprofit organizations. Contributions of cash and property to qualified organizations can be deductible for individual income tax purposes. Additionally, corporations can claim a limited deduction for charitable contributions made in cash or property.

Under the U.S. Internal Revenue Code (the IRC), organizations that are organized and operated for exempt purposes may qualify for tax-exempt status. Organizations qualifying for tax-exempt status are exempt from paying federal income taxes. Usually, federal tax exemption will also trigger tax exemption at the state and local level. Organizations may also be exempt from sales tax and property tax.[64]

The IRC recognizes several different types of nonprofit organizations. About half of nonprofit organizations in the U.S. are exempt under Section 501(c)(3) of the IRC. Charitable organizations qualifying for Section 501(c)(3) status include nonprofits organized for charitable, educational, religious, scientific, literary or cultural purposes.[65] Contributions made to 501(c)(3) organizations can be tax-deductible to the donor, up to specified limits. The IRC also offers federal tax exemption to foundations (grant making organizations), civic leagues, labor and agricultural organizations, chambers of commerce, veterans' organizations and additional types of organizations.

Nonprofit organizations provide a variety of services that federal, state and local governments in the U.S. might otherwise be required to offer. By providing tax exemptions, governments support the work of nonprofits and receive a direct benefit. Tax exemptions help qualifying nonprofit organizations pursue difficult, long-standing issues that would be challenging or impossible for a for-profit entity to pursue on an on-going basis.

---

[64] Nonprofit organizations are subject to tax on Unrelated Business Taxable Income (UBTI). UBTI is income from a regularly maintained trade or business that is carried on by the organization and does not further the organization's exempt purpose (other than by generating income). Income generated by a museum gift shop is an example of UBTI.

[65] To achieve and maintain tax-exempt status under Section 501(c)(3), organizations must comply with specific limitations and restrictions. These include limitations on unrelated business activities, private benefits and lobbying and a prohibition on political campaign activities.

Culture and Tradition

Culture and tradition play an important role in encouraging volunteering and charitable activity in the United States. The tradition of charitable activity runs deep in U.S. culture. People have been volunteering and helping each other much longer than the United States has been a country. Volunteering and charitable activity long predate any formal government policy. Given the long tradition of charitable activity in the U.S., perhaps it is not surprising that people continue to be so generous with their time and money today.

Individual Example and Leadership

Through their leadership, insight and example, a number of individuals have also played an important role in helping give shape to the nonprofit sector as it exists in the United States today. There is a long history of inspired leadership in the nonprofit sector. Philanthropists have made major donations to address fundamental issues like health, literacy and economic opportunity. Nonprofit executives have brought an increasingly professional, result-orientated approach to managing nonprofit organizations. Together, these people and others provide an important example and inspiration to the tens of millions of people in the U.S. who volunteer and make charitable donations every year.[66]

Charitable Policies and Practices in Other Countries

The United States is not the only country with a well-established nonprofit sector and a deeply-rooted tradition of charitable activity. A number of countries have legal, tax and policy frameworks in place encouraging the growth and development of nonprofit and charitable organizations. Some of these policy frameworks are more extensive than others. Additionally, the percentage of people who give money and give time to charitable causes in a number of countries is relatively high (and similar to the percentage in the U.S.).[67] Newly wealthy individuals and members of rapidly growing middle classes are also expressing increased interest in

---

[66] For additional commentary on philanthropy and individual example, see Edition #8 (December 17, 2012) of my newsletter.

[67] Based on data from the Charities Aid Foundation's World Giving Index (December 2013).

charitable activity in many countries.

The results of surveys conducted in 135 countries by Gallup for Charities Aid Foundation illustrate the breadth of participation in charitable activities worldwide. The practice of donating money to charity is widespread among the people of many countries, regardless of the level of economic development of a country. Ranked in terms of the percentage of their population who donate money to charity, eight of the top ten countries are not members of the Group of Twenty leading economies.[68] Similarly, the rate of participation in volunteering is also high in many countries.

Economic development, wealth creation and demographic trends suggest that interest in volunteering and charitable activities should also be higher in many countries in the future. As new wealth is created in a number of countries, there appears to be a corresponding increase in interest among newly wealthy individuals in making charitable donations. Additionally, as large numbers of people advance economically and join the middle class, there appears to be an increased interest on their part in volunteering.

Laws and policies of countries outside of the United States relating to nonprofit and charitable organizations will be examined in greater detail in a future edition of this newsletter.

How Countries and Policymakers Can Promote the Development of Nonprofit and Charitable Organizations

There are a variety of lessons that policymakers can learn from the experience of the United States and other countries with nonprofit organizations in order to help promote the development of dynamic and well-governed nonprofit sectors in their home countries. Worthwhile, quality policymaking requires an understanding of the bigger picture and an appreciation of how laws, policies, institutions, culture and individual behavior interact. A number of factors work together to help create a vibrant and successful nonprofit sector.

In order to help encourage the growth and development of a successful nonprofit sector, policymakers should consider the following:

---

[68] Burma was the country with the largest percentage of its people donating money to charity (85%). World Giving Index (December 2013).

- <u>Laws, Policies and Institutions</u>. Policymakers should review the current state of their laws and policies regarding nonprofit and charitable organizations and revise them as appropriate to encourage the development of transparent and accountable nonprofits. Corporate laws should be written specifically for not-for-profit entities. Policymakers should also address the continuing process of developing the institutions and expertise necessary to develop and support a well-governed nonprofit sector. Potential donors are much more comfortable giving their time and money to charitable organizations that are open and transparent about their activities and finances.

- <u>Tax Policy and Tax Incentives</u>. Policymakers should consider adopting tax incentives to encourage individuals and organizations to make charitable donations. Tax incentives play an important role in encouraging individuals, corporations and others to donate hundreds of billions of dollars to nonprofit organizations in the United States every year. While it is difficult to quantify with precision, it appears that the U.S. is receiving significantly more in the value of goods and services provided by nonprofit and charitable organizations than it is forgoing in potential tax revenue.

- <u>Culture and Tradition</u>. A deeply-rooted tradition of charitable activity is not unique to United States culture. The rate of participation in charitable acts and volunteering is high in a number of countries. Policymakers should work to create and strengthen laws, policies and institutions to help individuals direct their charitable aspirations in constructive and meaningful ways.

- <u>Individual Example and Leadership</u>. Through their leadership and example, nonprofit leaders, philanthropists, volunteers and others play an important role in encouraging many additional people to volunteer and perform charitable acts. With the creation of significant new wealth in a number of countries, there appears to be a corresponding increase in interest among newly wealthy individuals in making charitable donations and providing leadership to nonprofits. Additionally, with millions and millions of people joining the middle class worldwide, there appears to be increased interest in volunteering. By creating and strengthening laws and policies that encourage individuals to provide an example through their charitable donations and organizational leadership, policymakers also help make the broader growth of volunteering and charitable activity more possible.

Creating a successful nonprofit sector is a complex process that requires the active involvement of government, the private sector, the nonprofit sector and individuals. The factors discussed above work together to help create an environment in which people are comfortable with giving their time and money to charitable causes and organizations. These factors also help create an environment in which nonprofits can thrive and flourish as individual organizations on an on-going basis. Creating a successful nonprofit sector benefits a country in numerous ways.

NONPROFIT ORGANIZATIONS AND A COUNTRY'S BIGGER PICTURE

The Nonprofit Sector: A New Source of Economic Dynamism

Encouraging the development of a country's nonprofit sector can be valuable for a number of reasons. Nonprofit and charitable organizations provide social services that might otherwise need to be provided by the state.[69] Nonprofits create jobs. Nonprofits promote community building. There are additional benefits as well. By fostering the development of a robust, well-governed nonprofit sector, policymakers can help a country strengthen its broader legal and institutional framework, diversify its economy and develop an additional source of economic dynamism.

The potential of a well-developed nonprofit sector to contribute to a country's bigger picture is something that should not be underestimated. As noted above, nonprofit organizations are an important source of job creation and wage growth in the United States. Nonprofits play an important role in many leading economic sectors. Nonprofits are increasingly being managed in a professional, results-orientated manner. Additionally, interest in volunteering and other charitable activities is widespread worldwide. Given the economic and social benefits that a well-organized nonprofit sector can provide, policymakers are well advised to closely examine creating and strengthening the laws, policies and institutions necessary for a successful nonprofit sector.

---

[69] With government debt levels increasing and populations aging in many countries, it is possible that policymakers in more countries will want to look to organizations like nonprofits to help provide social services in the future.

WARREN BUFFETT'S ANNUAL LETTER
TO SHAREHOLDERS OF BERKSHIRE HATHAWAY

Commemorating 50 Years

The Value of Continually Refining How You Invest

The Value of Culture

BUILDING COMPANIES TO SUCCEED

Fifty years ago Warren Buffett took control of a textile company named Berkshire Hathaway. In the years following, he built that small company into a diversified conglomerate that employs 340,499 people and whose stock price has appreciated 1,826,163%.[70] It is an incredible record.

To commemorate the 50 years Warren Buffett has led Berkshire Hathaway, Buffett and Charles Munger have written a special annual letter to shareholders. In their most recent annual letter, Buffett and Munger share their thoughts on the past 50 years and the next 50 years for Berkshire Hathaway. As Buffett and Munger describe it, the investment approach underlying the success of Berkshire Hathaway has evolved significantly over the past 50 years. They also discuss the roles focus and culture have played in making Berkshire Hathaway the distinctive company it is today. In this edition of my newsletter, I discuss a few of the lessons about

---

[70] Data are from Warren Buffett's most recent annual letter. Warren Buffett's annual letter to shareholders of Berkshire Hathaway for the year 2014 is available at: http://www.berkshirehathaway.com/letters/2014ltr.pdf. The complete 2014 Berkshire Hathaway annual report is available at: http://www.berkshirehathaway.com/2014ar/2014ar.pdf.

building companies to succeed that can be learned from the annual letter and from their comments at the May 2 annual meeting.[71] Also, I am pleased to announce the publication of my new book.

WARREN BUFFETT'S ANNUAL LETTER

The Value of Continually Refining How You Invest

The investment style upon which Berkshire Hathaway has been built has evolved over the years. As Buffett notes in the annual letter, he initially pursued a value-focused approach of investing in "cigar-butt" companies:

> My cigar-butt strategy worked very well while I was managing small sums. Indeed, the many dozens of free puffs I obtained in the 1950s made that decade by far the   best of my life for both relative and absolute investment performance.

But cigar-butt investing had its limits. Investing in small companies that traded at bargain prices was "scalable only to a point." It would not work well for investing larger and larger amounts of money. Additionally, cigar-butt investing did not create a strong foundation upon which to build a large company capable of continuing to grow over the long term.

As the limitations of cigar-butt investing became more apparent, Buffett's investment philosophy evolved. Buffett writes:

> It took Charlie Munger to break my cigar-butt habits and set the course for building a business that could combine huge size with satisfactory profits.

Munger's insight was to invest in "wonderful businesses at fair prices" rather than "fair businesses at wonderful prices." By investing this way, Buffett and Munger were able to invest significantly larger amounts of money profitably. This insight provided the basis for the ongoing growth we continue to see at Berkshire Hathaway.

Over time, Buffett and Munger's investment style took on a number of additional refinements as well. The investment in See's Candy provided

---

[71] Full disclosure: I am a big fan of Warren Buffett and Charles Munger and a shareholder of Berkshire Hathaway.

valuable insight into the value of investing in well-established brands. Buffett and Munger also broadened their investment style to include large investments in companies in a variety of industries with very different economic characteristics, including insurance, finance, manufacturing, service and consumer brands, utilities, housing, newspapers and a railroad system.

Today Berkshire Hathaway is a highly-diversified conglomerate with investments in dozens of business sectors and major equity positions in leading Fortune 500 companies. Buffett notes that "Berkshire now owns 9½ companies that would be listed on the Fortune 500 were they independent (Heinz is the ½.)" As illustrated by the relatively recent purchases of BNSF Railway, the H.J. Heinz Company and Kraft Foods Group, Inc., Buffett and Munger's investment style continues to evolve and expand.

Markets, businesses and investing have all changed dramatically over the past 50 years. In spite of these dramatic changes, Berkshire Hathaway has continued to grow and expand. One important lesson to be learned from the history of Berkshire Hathaway is the value of continual learning and of continuing to refine how you invest.

The Value of Focus

The success of Berkshire Hathaway is built upon a number of important investment and business insights. In addition to Buffett and Munger's insight on the value of investing in quality companies and well-established brands, these insights include a nuanced understanding of the value of "float,"[72] the value of a conglomerate structure and the value of a conservative balance sheet. Each of these insights shares one characteristic in common: they are all the result of Buffett and Munger spending a considerable amount of time reading and thinking.

Thus, a second important lesson to be learned from the history of Berkshire Hathaway is the value of focus.

Charles Munger writes:

---

[72] In the insurance industry, "float" is used to describe money that is collected up front as premiums and invested before any losses are paid.

> … Buffett's decision to limit his activities to a few kinds and to maximize his attention to them, and to keep doing so for 50 years, was a lollapalooza.

As Munger notes in the annual letter, Buffett has focused on a relatively short list of primary activities. These activities include managing investments, choosing the Chief Executive Officers of important operating subsidiaries, allocating capital, making himself available for consultation with the CEOs of subsidiaries, writing a long and educational annual letter,[73] and, probably most importantly, being an exemplar of Berkshire Hathaway's culture and reserving much time for quiet reading and thinking. Munger also observes that Berkshire Hathaway has been very consciously organized and managed (a small conglomerate headquarters staff, "very extreme autonomy" for the CEOs of subsidiaries) to permit Buffett to focus on these primary activities.

By focusing on a short list of primary activities for such a long period of time, Buffett has been able to build upon and refine his principle strengths and the strengths of what Munger calls "the Berkshire system." Buffett's disciplined focus has produced a variety of valuable insights that have built upon each other and grown in value over the years, enabling Berkshire Hathaway to evolve and grow into the huge, highly-diversified conglomerate it is today. The results for Berkshire Hathaway have been growth in per-share book value at a rate of 19.4% compounded annually over the last 50 years[74] and a "lollapalooza."

The Value of Culture

The culture of an organization is very much a reflection of the people

---

[73] Buffett's practice of writing an annual letter has probably contributed to the success of Berkshire Hathaway more than many people realize. Writing an annual letter has permitted Buffett to educate shareholders, subsidiary managers and others about his investment and business practices (thus helping build a stable investor base, among other things), to communicate the types of investments he is seeking and to help reinforce Berkshire Hathaway's distinctive culture. Writing an annual letter is hard work. It forces the writer to clarify his or her own thinking and priorities, which leads to better focus and results. Everyone would benefit from writing an annual letter, even if it is written only to their family or to themselves.

[74] See page 3 of the Berkshire Hathaway annual letter.

leading it. Thus, what Buffett and Munger write about the qualities that a future CEO should have says much about the distinctive culture of Berkshire Hathaway.

"Character is crucial," Buffett writes. "A Berkshire CEO must be 'all in' for the company, not for himself." The example a CEO sets has a huge influence on the people a CEO leads and manages. "If it's clear to them that shareholders' interests are paramount to him, they will, with few exceptions, also embrace that way of thinking."

The primary responsibilities of a future CEO of Berkshire Hathaway will be allocating capital and selecting and retaining managers to lead the company's operating subsidiaries, Buffett writes. These duties will require that Berkshire Hathaway's CEO "be a rational, calm and decisive individual who has a broad understanding of business and good insights into human behavior." Buffett notes that his successor will also need the ability to fight off "arrogance, bureaucracy and complacency." Buffett writes that he feels that the very high level of delegation of authority at Berkshire Hathaway is "the ideal antidote to bureaucracy."

To help ensure the continuation of the company's distinctive culture, Buffett has suggested that his son, Howard Buffett, succeed him as non-executive Chairman of Berkshire Hathaway. Buffett writes that he suggested that Howard Buffett be made Chairman "to make change easier if the wrong CEO should ever be employed and there occurs a need for the Chairman to move forcefully." Buffett notes that he thinks there is a *very* *low probability*" of this issue arising at Berkshire Hathaway, but he adds that it is difficult to remove a CEO if that person is also Chairman. "The deed usually gets done, but almost always very late."

The distinctive culture that Buffett has developed at Berkshire Hathaway plays an important role in the company's continuing growth. One important component of the culture is the high degree of autonomy with which the managers of the company's operating subsidiaries operate. By being able to delegate heavily to operating managers, Buffett is able to focus much of his time on a few key value-creating activities. A third important lesson to be learned from the history of Berkshire Hathaway is the role corporate culture can play in company growth and value creation.

BUILDING COMPANIES TO SUCCEED

Berkshire Hathaway has changed significantly since Warren Buffett first took control of the company 50 years ago. What was once a struggling textile company is now a huge, successful and highly-diversified conglomerate. The phenomenal growth of Berkshire Hathaway is the result of a number of factors, including intelligent investing, disciplined focus, highly capable managers and a distinctive culture.

While it may not be possible to emulate what Charles Munger calls "the Berkshire system" in all respects, there is much to be learned from Buffett and Munger's annual letter and the history and future plans for Berkshire Hathaway. Three of the most important lessons to be taken from the annual letter are the following:

The first lesson is the value of continual learning. Businesses and markets have changed fundamentally in the five decades since Buffett bought Berkshire Hathaway. During this period, Buffett and Munger have made significant changes to the way in which they invest and manage their business. This ability to evolve and adapt has proven to be one of the keys to Berkshire Hathaway's success. Given the increasingly fast pace at which business, technology and global linkages are changing, it will become increasingly important for companies and individuals to continually learn and to adapt to change.

The second lesson is the value of focus. As Munger describes in the annual letter, Buffett has focused his considerable intellect on a relatively short and well-chosen list of priority activities for a very long time. The result of Buffett's highly disciplined focus has been a series of investment and business insights and business decisions that have built upon each other and enabled Berkshire Hathaway to grow into the huge, successful conglomerate it is today. To succeed in an increasingly competitive and global marketplace, companies and individuals need to have a very clear sense of their priorities, goals and objectives.

The third lesson is the value of culture. Buffett and Munger have developed a distinctive culture at Berkshire Hathaway. This culture is based upon the example set by Buffett, Munger and the leaders of Berkshire Hathaway's operating subsidiaries. One central element of the culture is the high degree of autonomy with which managers of the company's operating subsidiaries manage their businesses. By being able to delegate heavily to operating managers, Buffett is able to focus on a few key priority activities (including capital allocation, advising managers and new investments) where he can add the most value. Corporate culture can play an important role in company growth and value creation.

The lessons that can be learned from the growth and success of Berkshire Hathaway have much wider application than just to business. Lessons like the value of continual learning, focus and culture are as important to the success of countries, communities, families and individuals as they are to companies. No doubt many of the more than 40,000 people who attended the Berkshire Hathaway annual meeting in Omaha May 2 appreciate this point.

WARREN BUFFETT'S ANNUAL LETTER
TO SHAREHOLDERS OF BERKSHIRE HATHAWAY

"America's Economic Magic Remains Alive and Well"

Buffett and Munger's Blueprint for Building Berkshire Hathaway's Per-Share Intrinsic Value

The Value of Creating An Organization Where People Want to Work

NEW PODCAST

In this edition of my newsletter, I highlight three noteworthy insights from Warren Buffett's most recent annual letter to shareholders of Berkshire Hathaway. There may be a "negative drumbeat" on this year's campaign trail, Buffett writes. But "that view is dead wrong: The babies being born in America today are the luckiest crop in history."[75] Buffett explains why America's economy will continue to grow and the economic "pie to be shared by the next generation will be *far* larger than today's." He also offers an example of a clearly-defined set of objectives that helps Berkshire Hathaway managers keep focused on maximizing results and shows why creating an organization where people want to work can be so valuable.[76]

---

[75] Warren Buffett's annual letter to shareholders of Berkshire Hathaway for the year 2015 is available at: http://www.berkshirehathaway.com/letters/2015ltr.pdf. The complete 2015 Berkshire Hathaway annual report is available at: http://www.berkshirehathaway.com/2015ar/2015ar.pdf.

[76] Full disclosure: I am a big fan of Warren Buffett and Charles Munger and a shareholder of Berkshire Hathaway.

With this edition of my newsletter, I am pleased to announce the launch of my new podcast series. In my podcast, I discuss important, timely front page business and legal issues and interview thoughtful, inspiring people. To listen to my podcast, please go to: http://www.tlfraser.com/#!podcasts/c4m.

WARREN BUFFETT'S ANNUAL LETTER

"America's Economic Magic Remains Alive and Well"

One of the reasons Warren Buffett has been such a successful investor and business manager over the years is because he is able to place current events in a larger perspective. Observations he makes in his most recent annual letter are a good example:

> It's an election year, and candidates can't stop speaking about our country's problems (which, of course, only *they* can solve). As a result of this negative drumbeat, many Americans now believe that their children will not live as well as they themselves do.

> That view is dead wrong: The babies being born in America today are the luckiest crop in history.

Buffett observes that GDP per capita in the U.S. is *in real terms* six times the amount it was in 1930, the year he was born. This growth is attributable to a market system that enables U.S. citizens to work far more efficiently and produce far more today than they did in 1930. Not only does the U.S. economy produce far more goods and services than it did in the past, it also produces new goods and services that revolutionize the way people live. Through the power of compounding, even the U.S.'s current 2% per year growth in real GDP ("yes, we would all like to see a higher rate") delivers "astounding gains" over a generation.

While acknowledging that how GDP growth is divided in the U.S. "will remain fiercely contentious," he states that "the pie to be shared by the next generation will be *far* larger than today's."

"America's kids will live far better than their parents did."

A fundamentally important point to keep in mind during the current campaign season is that America's underlying economic system is fundamentally sound. Yes, there will be ups and downs in the economy in the future just like there have been in the past. Yes, some parts of the U.S. economy will experience fluctuations and changes much more than others. And yes, how the increased wealth is divided between people will continue to be contentious. But the point to remember is that the U.S. economy is fundamentally strong and adaptable.

Given the robustness of the U.S. economy, business leaders, nonprofit leaders, entrepreneurs, philanthropists, policymakers and others should continue to be decisive and move forward with purpose, focus, resolve and optimism. American's best days lie ahead.

Buffett and Munger's Blueprint for Building Berkshire Hathaway's Per-Share Intrinsic Value

Buffett sets out the "blueprint" for building Berkshire Hathaway's per-share intrinsic value and maximizing results in his annual letter. Buffett describes the blueprint as follows:

> (1) constantly improving the basic earning power of our many subsidiaries;
>
> (2) further increasing their earnings through bolt-on acquisitions;
>
> (3) benefiting from the growth of our investees;
>
> (4) repurchasing Berkshire shares when they are available at a meaningful discount from intrinsic value; and
>
> (5) making an occasional large acquisition.

Additionally, Buffett notes that Berkshire Hathaway will rarely, if ever, issue new shares.

Buffett's blueprint for building value and maximizing results is an excellent example of how a CEO can help managers and others in an organization focus on what is really important. Berkshire Hathaway might be a highly-diversified conglomerate employing more than 300,000 people, but Berkshire Hathaway is also a very focused company. Warren Buffett and Charles Munger think long and hard about priorities, goals and objectives for the organization. This focus is communicated to managers and employees through Buffett's annual letters, the blueprint for building value and in additional ways.

To accomplish ambitious goals in business, government, philanthropy and life, it is important to have clear, well-thought-through goals and objectives and to engage others in achieving them. Buffett's blueprint for building Berkshire Hathaway's per-share intrinsic value and maximizing results is an excellent example of communicating priorities, goals and objectives.

The Value of Creating An Organization Where People Want to Work

Buffett concludes his most recent annual letter with two pictures. The first picture is a picture of Buffett and the 24 men and women who work with him at corporate headquarters taken from the 2014 Berkshire Hathaway annual report. The second picture is also a picture of the headquarters team, taken one year later. The second picture is a picture of the same 25 people.

"Can you imagine another very large company – we employ 361,270 people worldwide – enjoying that kind of employment stability at headquarters?" Buffett writes.

Employment stability at corporate headquarters is, no doubt, one of many reasons why Berkshire Hathaway is the successful company it is. The 24 people who work with Buffett in the Omaha office are incredibly productive and efficient. As Buffett notes, they file a 30,400 page Federal income tax return, oversee the filing of 3,530 state tax returns, prepare the annual report, respond to numerous shareholder and media inquiries, prepare for a very large annual meeting (more than 40,000 people last year) and complete a number of additional projects and tasks.

The fact that employees stay at Berkshire Hathaway and are productive and efficient says a lot about the organization and its management. Hiring is being done well. Talented, capable people are being put in well-defined roles and given the opportunity to make a big contribution. Knowing Berkshire Hathaway's culture, I do not doubt that Buffett and other senior managers are also showing employees appreciation like Buffett does in his annual letters to his "All-Star" operating managers. With a highly capable headquarters team firmly in place, Buffett and other senior managers are able to spend a greater percentage of their time on priority activities, including managing investments and capital allocation and consulting with the CEOs of subsidiaries.

_____

The Berkshire Hathaway annual meeting is April 30 in Omaha. I will be attending the annual meeting and participating in book events this weekend. For information about the book events, please see my website closer to the date. If you will be in Omaha and would like to meet for coffee, please let me know.

NEW PODCAST

With this edition of my newsletter, I am pleased to announce the launch of my new podcast series. In my podcast, I discuss timely, important front page business and legal issues and interview thoughtful, inspiring people. One purpose of my podcast is to help listeners understand the significance of current issues and how insights from the front pages can be applied to their business and personal lives in valuable ways.

In a special edition of my podcast, I talk with Jim Ross, manager of the Hudson Booksellers bookstore at Eppley Airport in Omaha, Nebraska, about books Warren Buffett and Charles Munger read and about how their reading habits have contributed to their phenomenal success. In initial episodes of my podcast, I have also discussed innovation and brand building in China, Google's reorganization as a holding company and Jack Ma's letter to shareholders of Alibaba.

Expect to hear interviews with some very interesting people in coming weeks in my podcast.

To listen to my podcast, please go to:
http://www.tlfraser.com/#!podcasts/c4m.

THE BUFFETT GENRE:
TALKING BOOKS WITH JIM ROSS

The Podcast Interview

A WARREN BUFFETT AND CHARLES MUNGER
BOOK LIST

In a special episode of my podcast, I talk with Jim Ross, proprietor of the Hudson Booksellers bookstore at Eppley Airport in Omaha, Nebraska, about books Warren Buffett and Charles Munger read and about how their reading habits have contributed to their phenomenal success.

As proprietor of the Omaha bookstore for 20 years, Ross has thoughtful insight into the authors and books admired by Buffett and Munger (and the books read by the thousands and thousands of shareholders, business leaders, academics and others who come through his bookstore during the weekend of the Berkshire Hathaway annual meeting and throughout the year).

THE PODCAST INTERVIEW

Hello. I'm Tom Fraser and this is a special edition of my podcast. Today I am in Omaha, Nebraska, at Omaha's Eppley Airport. If you walk with me to the north end of the terminal, and take the escalator up to the second floor, you will see a Hudson Booksellers bookstore. I am standing in the bookstore with Jim Ross, the store's proprietor. We are surrounded by a large collection of books about Warren Buffett, Charles Munger and Berkshire Hathaway. As you are about to learn, this is no ordinary bookstore.

Jim, I understand that your bookstore gets pretty busy the weekend of

the Berkshire Hathaway annual meeting. What does the scene look like then?

The weekend of the Berkshire Hathaway annual meeting is our Christmas. We do 17 to 18 percent of our business during the three days that shareholders come in from around the world for the meeting. It's an incredible time for us. As one of my booksellers said … you get to meet the richest, wisest people in the world during those three days. We decided, many years ago actually, to cater to this crowd. We always have had a collection of books relating to Berkshire Hathaway, to value investing, to [Benjamin] Graham, to Buffett, to Munger and to everything connected with Berkshire.

I'm really curious … how did you assemble your collection of Buffett books? I understand it's a pretty big collection.

We have between 40 and 50 titles connected with Berkshire Hathaway. It's evolved over the years. It started about 18 years ago. I've been with the bookstore 20 years. We would have an onslaught of people after the annual meeting coming in and asking for particular titles. People would come into the bookstore and say "Do you have this book?" It was actually people coming from the meeting looking for a book that either Mr. Buffett or Mr. Munger had brought up in the middle of the meeting. These were brilliant books. These were books you would normally have on hand, but you wouldn't have 200 of them.

It was months after one of the shareholder meetings that I ran into Mr. Buffett. I explained to him our dilemma that we would have crowds of people looking for specific titles. He said that the last time they had had that sort of interest it was a book that Charlie had recommended. He said, "I will give you Charlie's telephone number. Ninety days before the meeting, you call Charlie and he will tell you what we're reading." I was flabbergasted. He gave me the phone number. I called. What shocked me was that he [Munger] immediately answered the phone. I thought we were going to go through at least four or five executive assistants. Charlie said, "This is Charlie." And I could not complete a sentence. I was lost. I think I got out my name. He interrupted me in my fumbling and said, "I know who you are. I know why you're calling. How can I help you?"

That year Charlie was interested in Ron Chernow's book ***Titan*** [***Titan: The Life of John D. Rockefeller, Sr.***], which is a biography of Rockefeller. He was also very big on ***Guns, Germs and Steel*** [***Guns, Germs, and Steel: The Fates of Human Societies***]. He's always been a huge fan of Jared Diamond. We talked for 15 minutes. We had a wonderful conversation and he said those were the books that they would be talking about if it came up. That was another thing ... when I first mentioned it to Mr. Buffett, he said, "Jim, what if no one asks what we're reading?" I said, "Fat chance. Someone always asks." He was concerned I would be stuck with piles of books. I had to explain that books are returnable. So we wouldn't be stuck with them. That's when he decided to give me Mr. Munger's telephone number. And it just went from there. So, when the first meeting came along, he not only mentioned ***Guns, Germs and Steel*** and ***Titan*** ... he endorsed the store ... Charlie did. We were very pleased.

Buffett and Munger's book list is long and diverse. The books are not just about value investing. What other types of titles are included in the book list?

There are a lot of biographies. Buffett is a big fan of Katharine Graham's autobiography [***Personal History***], which is a terrific book. And Charlie has interests that are so broad ... including things like physics. There's a great book out called ***Seeking Wisdom from Darwin to Munger*** [Peter Bevelin]. I was able to show him the manuscript when the author was working on it. It is basically an overview of great thinkers. It is in honor of both Munger and Buffett. Even though he only has Munger's name in the title, there is a lot of Buffett in that book. It really shows the breadth of their reading. It's phenomenal. They read everything. They read every day. It's always been amazing to me [how much they read].

A lot of my listeners have attended Berkshire Hathaway meetings in the past, so I am curious ... can you give us a scoop? Are there any new titles that people should be looking for?

I usually talk to Mr. Munger before the meeting. I haven't talked to him yet. So I can't give you any big scoop right now. Larry Cunningham has a new book on the essays of Warren Buffett that came out in November. [***The Essays of Warren Buffett: Lessons for Corporate America, Fourth Edition.***]

Well, check back to my website in a couple of months. I will add new book titles there as we learn more. I would like to talk about Buffett and Munger a bit more. Why are people so fascinated with Buffett and Munger?

Their success, their amazing success, is one obvious reason why people are so interested. Another reason would have to be that they are who you see. We have people who come in the store all the time who assume that he doesn't really live in Omaha. That he must live in some exotic locale. We say to them … Mr. Buffett actually lives up the street from me, he pumps his own gas, he drives his own car. There's no pretense about him at all. He is exactly who he is in front of the public. They are terrific people. I don't want to give the impression that I socialize with them on a regular basis or anything like that. But they are who you see and I think that's part of the fascination. They are regular guys.

Jim, you grew up in Omaha. Warren Buffett grew up in Omaha. Charles Munger grew up in Omaha. How did Omaha shape who Buffett and Munger are today?

Good Midwestern values. That sounds cliché. There is a great book out on this by Steve Jordon, who is one of the editors of the **Omaha World-Herald.** *The Oracle & Omaha.* **[***The Oracle & Omaha: How Warren Buffett and His Hometown Shaped Each Other.***]** It's about how Buffett was shaped by Omaha. It's also about how Omaha, quite frankly, has been shaped by Buffett. It's a great book.

It talks about his beginnings. Everybody's heard the stories about the Coke bottles and working in the Buffett grocery store. His dad was a broker here locally. They were conservative, homespun people. And he still is. For a while he lived in New York. I grew up with Howie [Howard Buffett, Buffett's son] and I can remember Howie talking about when they decided to move back from New York. It was basically … I can do this anywhere. Let's go back to Omaha where I am going to be grounded and away from the cacophony. And the rest, as they say, is history.

What do you think Buffett represents to Omaha?

He's like a steady rock to the city ... and a steady influence. While other parts of the country might have large highs and lows, we've just never experienced that sort of thing. It's all very stable and pretty even. And that's what he represents. When he got together with his initial investors in the late fifties, he basically said to them I'm going to invest the money and we're going to have some returns. Don't bother me. Trust me and we'll go far with this. He was not flamboyant. The types of people he gathered around him as investors were that way too. They were all looking for a rock solid sort of investment, even though he wasn't really that proven at that point. But they trusted him … he showed them what he wanted to do … and it all flowered.

So, Buffett's steady, cerebral approach was very apparent when he was younger and he has steadily kept at it throughout the years. He has also been a steady reader.

Yes.

I would encourage everybody listening to this podcast to appreciate the tremendous value of steady, quality reading over time.

Yes.

Jim, this has been a lot of fun. I would like to thank you for taking time out of your busy day to speak to me and my listeners. If you would like to learn more about books about Warren Buffett, Charles Munger and Berkshire Hathaway, please go to my website: www.tlfraser.com. A list of books curated by Jim Ross will be posted there. And the next time you are at Eppley Airport in Omaha, Nebraska, please make a point of visiting Jim's store and coming in to say hello.

Editor's note. The above interview has been edited for purposes of clarity and brevity. The original podcast can be listened to in its entirety at: http://www.tlfraser.com/#!podcasts/c4m.

A Warren Buffett and Charles Munger Book List

Curated by Jim Ross, Hudson Booksellers

101 Reasons to Own the World's Greatest Investment: Warren Buffett's Berkshire Hathaway. Robert P. Miles.

1493: Uncovering the New World Columbus Created. Charles C. Mann.

Active Value Investing: Making Money in Range-Bound Markets. Vitaliy N. Katsenelson.

Art & Science of Value Investing: Invest Like Billionaire Warren Buffett. Scott Thompson.

Berkshire Beyond Buffett: The Enduring Value of Values. Lawrence A. Cunningham.

The Black Swan: The Impact of the Highly Improbable. Nassim Nicholas Taleb.

The Blind Watchmaker. Richard Dawkins.

Buffett: The Making of an American Capitalist. Roger Lowenstein.

Buffett's Bites: The Essential Investor's Guide to Warren Buffett's Shareholder Letters. L.J. Rittenhouse.

Charlie Munger: The Complete Investor. Tren Griffin.

The Clash of the Cultures: Investment vs. Speculation. John C. Bogle.

Common Sense on Mutual Funds: New Imperatives for the Intelligent Investor. John C. Bogle.

Common Stocks & Uncommon Profits. Philip A. Fisher.

Damn Right! Behind the Scenes with Berkshire Hathaway Billionaire Charlie Munger. Janet Lowe.

Dear Mr. Buffett: What an Investor Learns 1,269 Miles from Wall Street. Janet M. Tavakoli.

The Education of a Value Investor: My Transformative Quest for Wealth, Wisdom and Enlightenment. Guy Spier.

The End of Wall Street. Roger Lowenstein.

Entrepreneurs + Mentors = Success. Barnett C. Helzberg Jr.

The Essays of Warren Buffett: Lessons for Corporate America (Fourth Edition). Lawrence A. Cunningham.

A Few Lessons for Investors & Managers from Warren Buffett. Peter Bevelin.

The Financial Times Guide to Value Investing: How to Become a Disciplined Investor. Glen Arnold.

Foods You Will Enjoy – The Story of Buffett's Store. Bill Buffett.

Fooled by Randomness: The Hidden Role of Chance in Life and in the Markets. Nassim Nicholas Taleb.

Forty Chances: Finding Hope in a Hungry World. Howard G. Buffett.

The Four Filters Invention of Warren Buffett and Charles Munger. Bud Labitan.

Genome: The Autobiography of a Species in 23 Chapters. Matt Ridley.

Getting There: A Book of Mentors. Gillian Zoe Segal.

Giving It All Away: The Doris Buffett Story. Michael Zitz.

The Great Investors: Lessons on Investing from Master Traders. Glen Arnold.

The Great Minds of Investing. Hendrik Leber.

Guns, Germs & Steel: The Fates of Human Societies. Jared M. Diamond.

How the Scots Invented the Modern World: The True Story of How

Western Europe's Poorest Nation Created Our World & Everything In It. Arthur Herman.

How to Build a Business Warren Buffett Would Buy: The R.C. Willey Story. Jeff Benedict.

How to Pick Stocks Like Warren Buffett: Profiting from the Bargain Hunting Strategies of the World's Greatest Value Investor. Timothy Vick.

How to Start Your Very First Business (Warren Buffett's Secret Millionaires Club). Julie Merberg.

How to Think Like Benjamin Graham and Invest Like Warren Buffett. Lawrence A. Cunningham.

Influence: The Psychology of Persuasion. Robert B. Cialdini.

The Intelligent Investor. Benjamin Graham.

Investing Between the Lines: How to Make Smarter Decisions by Decoding CEO Communications. L.J. Rittenhouse.

Investing: The Last Liberal Art. Robert G. Hagstrom.

Investment Banking for Dummies. Matthew Krantz, Robert R. Johnson.

The Investment Checklist: The Art of In-Depth Research. Michael Shearn.

The Language Instinct: How the Mind Creates Language. Steven Pinker.

Life is What You Make It: Find Your Own Path to Fulfillment. Peter Buffett.

The Little Book of Sideways Markets: How to Make Money in Markets that Go Nowhere. Vitaliy N. Katsenelson.

Making Sense of the Fine Print: How Today's Front Page Legal Issues Impact Business, Policy and Personal Success. Thomas L. Fraser.

Man's Search for Meaning. Viktor E. Frankl.

A Master Class with Warren Buffett and Charlie Munger. Eben Otuteye, Mohammad Siddiquee.

A Matter of Degrees: What Temperature Reveals About the Past and Future of Our Species, Planet and Universe. Gino Segre.

The Most Important Thing Illuminated: Uncommon Sense for the Thoughtful Investor. Howard Marks.

My Warren Buffett Bible: A Short and Simple Guide to Rational Investing: 284 Quotes from the World's Most Successful Investor. Robert L. Bloch.

No Two Alike: Human Nature and Human Individuality. Judith Rich Harris.

Nuclear Terrorism: The Ultimate Preventable Catastrophe. Graham Allison.

The Nurture Assumption: Why Children Turn Out the Way They Do. Judith Rich Harris.

Of Permanent Value: The Story of Warren Buffett. Andrew Kilpatrick.

The Oracle & Omaha: How Warren Buffett and His Hometown Shaped Each Other. Steve Jordon.

Outliers: The Story of Success. Malcolm Gladwell.

The Outsiders: Eight Unconventional CEOs and Their Radically Rational Blueprint for Success. William N. Thorndike, Jr.

Personal History. Katharine Graham.

Poor Charlie's Almanack: The Wit and Wisdom of Charles T. Munger. Peter D. Kaufman.

The Real Warren Buffett: Managing Capital, Leading People. James O'Loughlin.

Securities Analysis. Benjamin Graham, David Dodd.

Seeking Wisdom: From Darwin to Munger. Peter Bevelin.

The Selfish Gene. Richard Dawkins.

The Snowball: Warren Buffett and the Business of Life. Alice Schroeder.

Strategic Value Investing: Practical Techniques of Leading Value Investors. Stephen Horan, Robert R. Johnson.

SuperFreakonomics: Global Cooling, Patriotic Prostitutes, and Why Suicide Bombers Should Buy Life Insurance. Steven Levitt, Stephen J. Dubner.

Tap Dancing to Work: Warren Buffett on Practically Everything, 1966-2013. Carol J. Loomis.

The Third Chimpanzee. Jared M. Diamond.

Titan: The Life of John D. Rockefeller, Sr. Ron Chernow.

Too Big to Fail: The Inside Story of How Wall Street and Washington Fought to Save the Financial System – and Themselves. Andrew Ross Sorkin.

A Universe from Nothing: Why There Is Something Rather than Nothing. Lawrence M. Krauss.

Warren Buffett: An Illustrated Biography of the World's Most Successful Investor. Ayano Morio.

The Warren Buffett CEO: Secrets from the Berkshire Hathaway Managers. Robert P. Miles.

Warren Buffett Portfolio: Mastering the Power of the Focus Investment Strategy. Robert G. Hagstrom.

Warren Buffett Speaks: Wit and Wisdom from the World's Greatest Investor. Janet Lowe.

Warren Buffett's Ground Rules: Words of Wisdom from the Partnership Letters of the World's Greatest Investor. Jeremy C. Miller.

The Wealth and Poverty of Nations: Why Some Are So Rich and Some Are So Poor. David S. Landes.

Where are the Customers' Yachts?: or A Good Hard Look at Wall Street. Fred Schwed Jr.

While America Aged: How Pension Debts Ruined General Motors, Stopped the NYC Subways, Bankrupted San Diego, and Loom as the Next Financial Crisis. Roger Lowenstein.

Why Moats Matter: The Morningstar Approach to Stock Investing. Heather Brilliant, Elizabeth Collins.

The Women of Berkshire Hathaway: Lessons from Warren Buffett's Female CEOs and Directors. Karen Linder.

Yes! 50 Scientifically Proven Ways to Be Persuasive. Noah J. Goldstein, Steve J. Martin, Robert B. Cialdini.

Thomas Fraser would like to thank Jim Ross, manager of the Hudson Booksellers bookstore at Eppley Airport in Omaha, Nebraska, for providing this book list.

ADDITIONAL INFORMATION

If you have questions or comments regarding the topics covered in these newsletters, or if you are interested in receiving copies of future newsletters, please contact Thomas L. Fraser at tom@tlfraser.com.

The author has made every effort to provide accurate Internet addresses at the time of writing. Websites may have expired or changed since the manuscript was prepared.

The information provided in this book does not constitute the provision of legal, tax or investment advice. This information is provided for general informational purposes only. Receipt of this information does not create an attorney-client relationship. An attorney-client relationship is not created until a written agreement has been reached to handle a particular matter. Readers should not act upon this without seeking advice from professional advisers. Prior results do not guarantee a similar outcome. Attorney advertising.

www.tlfraser.com

Editor's Note: The Additional Information section is included as a part of every newsletter, but is printed once in this book on this page in order to take out repetitive text.

ACKNOWLEDGMENTS

Writing a book on the topics of business, law and policy is, by its nature, a large, complex and collaborative project. Thus, I would like to thank the many people who have offered insight, wisdom and inspiration for this book and for my newsletter and podcast. I appreciate your questions, comments and observations. Your perceptive insight and original ideas inform my work and writing in many ways. I am fortunate to have you as clients, colleagues and friends. Chuan Lin, thank you for your excellent research. Jim Ross, thank you for your excellent insight on important and worthwhile books.

To my family, with love.

Thomas L. Fraser
New York City
April 7, 2016

INDEX